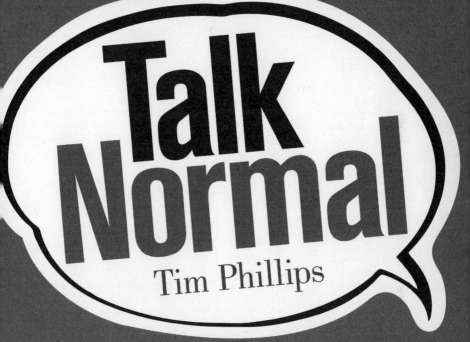

Talk Normal

Tim Phillips

STOP THE BUSINESS SPEAK, JARGON AND WAFFLE

KoganPage

LONDON PHILADELPHIA NEW DELHI

First published in Great Britain and the United States in 2011 by Kogan Page Limited

120 Pentonville Road	1518 Walnut Street, Suite 1100	4737/23 Ansari Road
London N1 9JN	Philadelphia PA 19102	Daryaganj
United Kingdom	USA	New Delhi 110002
www.koganpage.com		India

© Tim Phillips, 2011

ISBN   978 0 7494 6364 9
E-ISBN   978 0 7494 6365 6

British Library Cataloguing-in-Publication Data

A CIP record for this book is available from the British Library.

Library of Congress Cataloging-in-Publication Data

Phillips, Tim, 1967-
    Talk normal : stop the business speak, jargon and waffle / Tim Phillips.
        p. cm.
    Includes index.
    ISBN 978-0-7494-6364-9 – ISBN 978-0-7494-6365-6   1. Business communication.
2. Communication in management.   3. Jargon (Terminology)   I. Title.
    HF5718.P53 2011
    651.7–dc22
                                                                            2011016031

Typeset by Graphicraft Ltd, Hong Kong
Production managed by Jellyfish
Printed and bound in Great Britain by CPI Antony Rowe

Contents

Foreword

Talk Normal facilitates information delivery through multiple media formats and monetises eyeballs

London, UK, Mar 30, 2011/TalkNormalWire – Talk Normal (**http://talknormal.co.uk**), the leading solution for information clarity optimisation and humour-based jargon mitigation strategies, has announced that it will henceforth facilitate information delivery through multiple media formats.

The expanded service offering encompasses a paper-based added-value offering which leverages content originated in the pre-existing electronic service delivery method. Utilising multiple delivery channels matches eyeballs to content in an optimised and diversified platform: while retaining unity of purpose, the paper-based variant can reach Talk Normal partners who face electrical or data-access challenges, and additionally it interfaces with partners who want to make proactive moves to Talknormalise their jargon portfolios. It will also expedite the creation of enhanced revenue streams by monetising Talk Normal's attention endowment.

Talk Normal's chief solution advocate, Tim Phillips, commented that 'Many people ask me what this means to me. It means I've written a book about my blog so I can earn some money'.

Introduction

The blog that inspired this book was born out of frustration and, let's face it, anger. I can't dress it up as a pleasant emotion.

I have spent 20 years as a journalist, but not as one of the famous ones. I'm the sort that gets the opportunity to interview the deputy assistant director of sales for the Northern region, because the CEO has better things to do. I have to wade through the unfiltered thoughts of unreadable lawyers to work out what they just said, so I can interpret it for people for whom it really matters, but who don't speak fluent lawyer. I review thousands of words written for websites, and at the end have to call the person who commissioned me because I'm still not sure what the company actually does.

Talk Normal: why we bother

Like you, I'm swamped by e-mail, much of which I can't understand. I go to conferences where I can't keep my mind on the presentations, understand their diagrams, or work out what my 'take away' is. I take part in conference calls, where we can't say what we mean, though not for lack of time: Talk Normal readers report three-hour calls, which they use as an opportunity to tidy their desks or sharpen their pencils, occasionally brought back to earth when their opinions are sought on a conversation they haven't been following.

At this point, it's best to say that we should follow it up in a sidebar meeting, or take it offline. That's what these meetings are for: the opportunity for everyone to admit they weren't listening, after the boss has gone, and try to piece together what we missed. You don't need me to tell you that it shouldn't be like this.

Sometimes, trapped on a conference call that won't finish, I mute myself so I can scream with frustration loud enough to bring my wife running into my office, full of concern. Once I forgot to press the mute button: it wasn't just my wife that was worried for my well-being.

So I started to write a blog called Talk Normal for people who felt the same way. Many of my friends and colleagues, and some new acquaintances, joined in, and sometimes forwarded my posts to others, who subscribed, and e-mailed me to ask for a post on the thing that really, really irritated them.

They were confused by words that people around them used every day, and some of them admitted that they used the same words when they didn't know what they meant. They were bored at work, and when they went home they were driven crazy by salespeople. They shouted at the advertisements on their televisions, and at political robots on the radio who couldn't give a straight answer. They also wanted to do something about it, but didn't know where to start.

That's the point of this book. I've pulled out some of the problems, and interviewed some of the people who do a great job in solving them. I've included lots of things that have worked for me, when I have helped companies and individuals who came to me. And I've made fun of a lot of people – because there are a lot of people who deserve it.

Being a Talknormaliser has also made work more fun: people started to say to me: 'I hope you don't put this in your blog', after they'd said something particularly ridiculous. (I have made a point of including as much as I can. This may be, as the old joke puts it, one of the longest career suicides in history.) It gave me a reason to be interested in the dullest conversations, just in case there was something I could use. It even gave me a reason to use Twitter.

If you're a regular reader of the blog, you might recognise some of the content, repurposed and reordered. Other parts of it, especially the practical bits which try to help, are new. The book is roughly divided into sections on jargon, work, the media and marketing, with ideas on how to make your world better, but that doesn't mean you have to start at page 1.

The meaning of Talknormalism

The book uses my own insider jargon: Talknormalism and Talknormalisation. I've come up with three guiding principles, which seem to be sensible. I can't guarantee I always succeed, but I try, and I think others should too.

1. Try to be understood by everyone who's listening

When you're not, you create an 'in' group and an 'out' group, who can hear you, but not understand. That's always been a function of language – and of jargon especially. It conveys power and status on people who know the lingo. Or, if you prefer (I do), it robs the people who don't know what's going on of power and status.

We like to do this, because we are tribal. It also makes us feel comfortable to show off our knowledge, or to compete to see who knows the most in a meeting. It doesn't help the others.

Sometimes I train people to talk to journalists – or, more accurately, to talk to the people who journalists write for. Often they ask me to teach them about 'spin', a word I hate, because it makes deception sound smart.[1] I suggest that we try to find a way for them to communicate with people who are curious, but who aren't experts.

It is remarkable how many people, even in senior management positions, have never thought specifically about this. Maybe they have forgotten that non-experts exist, because as they spend more time at work, and more of their friends do the same job, and more people are afraid to admit that they don't understand, their 'in' group becomes their universe. They have no idea how small it is.

Talknormalisation expands that universe.

2. Stop trying to sound clever for no reason

The temptation to sound like a person who knows something isn't just damaging to you; it's insulting to real experts, who are often very good at using common language to make complex problems clear. Anyone can take a difficult thing and make it sound confusing. You don't need to be an expert to do that.

On the other hand, it's an understandable defensive reaction when you're under pressure. Often I find myself in a meeting where the conversation spirals off into technical gibberish, or disappears down an obscure rathole, because two people (it's a guy thing, admit it) are fighting for unspoken dominance.

You are not helping the rest of us live our lives.

3. It's about attitude, not rules

I'm constantly contacted by amateur grammarians who want me to post something about the abuse of dangling modifiers. I don't do this because I don't really know what a dangling modifier is. I could look it up on Wikipedia and pretend that I know what I'm talking about but that would mean I was trying to sound clever for no reason (see above).

We need to think clearly to write clearly, not swallow a book about grammar. I edit some terrible articles. The first thought is that there's a problem with the grammar: then when you fix the grammar you often find that there isn't a clear train of thought underlying what they wrote. That's the problem, not the dangling modifier.

Note

1   Renaming grubby deception-through-manipulation as clever 'spin' means that the word spin is an example of what it describes, like the word 'word'.

1 Trying to sound clever

Jargon: can't live with it, can't live without it

Memo to office bores, puffed-up marketers and blokes who rock on the balls of their feet while jingling the change in their pocket: say what you mean. Your jargon phrases, weasel words and waffle are doing our heads in.

And yet something about jargon is attractive. It makes us feel powerful, it makes us feel safe, and it makes us feel important. When we realise this, we can resist the temptation.

Accepting that we all have a problem is the first step to Talknormalisation.

We enjoy jargon too much

We treat jargon as an unfortunate by-product of the way we live, like lead poisoning, or flatulence. We don't like it, but individually we can't do anything about it; resignation is more often our approach than anger. So there are many surveys that list the words people hate, but far fewer plans to eliminate those words.

This is not just about making us happy: only a small minority of English speakers have English as a first language. If you want to communicate with as many people as possible – for example, if you're a government – then isn't it your responsibility to make your language accessible to all the people who need to understand you?

So quiet irritation is the commonly accepted response to day-to-day jargon. We're not supposed to slap people in the office – especially not because we disagree with their choice of adjective – and a combination of social pressure and hierarchy means we can't yell 'for the love of polysyllablism, shut up!' At least, not in board meetings. So we sit there, biting our tongues, waiting for the torture to end.

Nobody dies because of jargon – though many of us perish just a little bit, inside. It's not a crime to speak gobbledygook, but there isn't a jury in the land who wouldn't convict some of the managers I've met in the past 20 years of assaulting our ears. Jargon is rarely taken seriously enough to analyse systematically, although I have made some attempts in this book.[1]

This sense of helplessness in the face of jargon is made worse by its dullness. If you've ever been in a meeting and tuned out for a few minutes, only to come back to the room and find what seems like the same sentence meandering on, you know what I mean.

Occasionally, we even end up boring ourselves. I did this once on BBC Radio, and found the jargony point I was making so tedious that I completely lost track of what I was saying in the middle of a sentence, much to the surprise of my fellow studio guests. I must have sounded drunk. I was merely intoxicated by my own waffle.

A fashion for jargon

Jargon is often useful, when used between consenting adults. If I know what I mean by supply chain management, and you know what I mean by supply chain management, and we want to discuss the topics that we both correctly assume are covered by this shared assumption, let's call it supply chain management and to hell with everyone else. I'm not advocating a year zero approach to jargon, where we forget all our specialist knowledge and have to describe the wonderful things we do in some kind of pidgin English.

On the other hand, was there a time when we didn't have to listen to people in meetings telling us what to do with low-hanging fruit? Indeed there was, and it was more recent than you think.

Figure 1.1 Jargon's golden age: growth of three jargon phrases since 1990

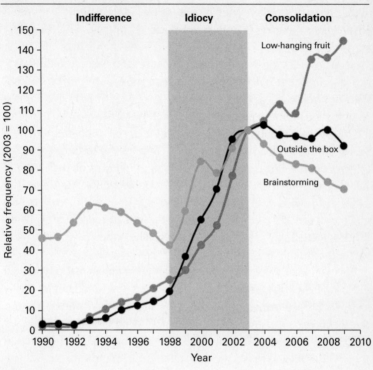

Source: Factiva

For a lot of the buzzword bingo-type words we hate, the real growth occurred in the late 1990s and early 2000s, rather than recently. Look at the graph (Figure 1.1) of how often low-hanging fruit, outside the box and brainstorming turn up in US publishing, adjusted so that their frequency in 1993 was 100 in each case. For these three, as for countless other jargon phrases like 'world class' or 'cutting edge', a period of slow growth during the early 1990s suddenly accelerates for five or six years. After 2003 or 2004, growth often stops.

The instruction to think 'outside the box', used as jargon for thinking creatively, was five times as common in 2003 as it had been in 1998. It's not like we were unfamiliar with the concept of creative thought until 1998 – or, for that matter, the concept of a box – so it looks like it's down to people trying to sound hip.

Some of today's most painful jargon was effectively non-existent in our lifetime. Until the mid-1990s no one wrote about low-hanging fruit (1990–92, seven newspaper articles mention it in the whole world), unless they were writing an article about the location of, well, fruit.

It's not shocking that this explosion in rubbish came at the same time as an explosion in the sort of businesspeople who spoke it. Some of you, lucky people, will be too young to recall the dot-com boom, where newspapers compared the twentysomething owners of websites to sell ski passes to the great entrepreneurs of history. With hindsight most of that generation of entrepreneurs were a bit rubbish at changing the world (though few were as loopy as the creators of the iSmell, effectively a printer for smells that we were all going to use to make our web browsing more aromatic), but they talked a lot about how they were going to do it.

For a short time many of us wanted to be like the dot-com kids, so we parroted the same c**ppy MBA jargon that they used. After 2003 the dot-commers mostly disappeared; but now apparently we can't stop ourselves from talking like them. The buzzwords the dot-commers left behind are the fag burns in the plush carpet of our language after a bulls**t orgy has been held on it. Thanks, guys.

Look closely at the shape of those three curves. Look also at the shape of the curve showing the frequency in US press releases of the jargon words which were considered most irritating by a group of writers, journalists and marketers (Figure 1.2).

I've drawn a straight line through them, which would be a simple regression, and a good fit. The simple point is that we're more than five times as likely to see these words in press releases today as we were in 1990, when the internet was something that people did in laboratories, and the dot-com entrepreneurs were precocious school-children who were obviously not disciplined often enough.

But from 2003 onwards, the curve flattens in both cases. Our jargon phrases have reached a saturation point. They have, perhaps, completed the first phase of joining the language, just as 'taken aback' was once jargon that only sailors would recognise.

A better fit might be a stretched letter 'S' – slow growth at first, followed by a rapid spread, followed by settling at a level. What spreads like this? Two things:

1 **Disease.** In this concept, we 'catch' jargon, rather like we
   catch Herpes. Not, of course, exactly like we catch Herpes,

Figure 1.2   Index of frequency of seven jargon phrases in US press releases, 1990–2009

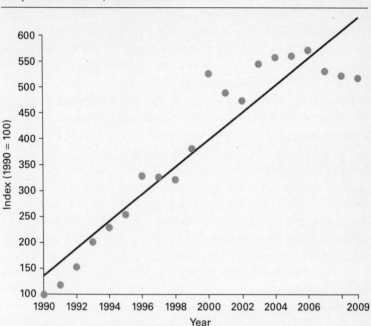

Source: Factiva

unless you work in a very sleazy office. In favour of this interpretation, this is how we like to think about ourselves: we are innocent victims. Someone coughs his world-class low-hanging fruit all over us, and before we know it, we're blurting it out on a conference call. It's true in some ways, but we're not powerless. Nobody tells us exactly what words to use when we are grown up.

2   **Haircuts.** Not just haircuts, but iPhones and hula hoops and pomegranate juice too. When there's something new, a group of trendsetters, or 'early adopters', pick it up. Research companies look for these people, because no matter how barmy the fad, they know that other people will copy it. So what's used, worn or bought by a few people one month is used, worn or bought by a few thousand, then a few million. Eventually, everyone who wants the haircut, has the right hair for it and wants to be seen in public with hair like that has the haircut.

I prefer the second interpretation. The group complaining about jargon (you, me, Talknormalisers everywhere) are like the people who thought the hula hoop was a waste of time. Others are picking up the jargon because it's rewarding – they like it. It gives them insider status. It signals knowledge (they assume) and makes them sound clever (they hope). It shows membership of an insider group, and stuff the rest of us.

If that's how you want to live, go ahead and live like that. Just please, please stop sending me your e-mails. I might catch something.

Catching jargon

There are phrases that are verbal tics that we seem to pick up easily from each other like a bad cold, especially those of us who live in closed, isolated communities. The public sector is often accused of this, with some justification (Figure 1.3).[2]

I'm delighted for the population of Harrow, but I suppose we must spare a thought for the traffic wardens: I'd much rather be a civil enforcement officer; it sounds dangerous and exciting. Yet the public sector is not the only offender. In fact, as this shows, the only formal initiatives I can find to Talknormalise our daily lives come from the government. About time too, but there's no reason for business to be smug.

Reverse the loss situation

As MG Rover gradually coasted to a stop in 2003, Kevin Howe, the group chief executive of Phoenix Venture Holdings, told the press that 'Going forward we will remain focused on continuing to reverse the loss situation.' Howe had a grasp of gobbledygook that one doesn't often see, even in a group chief executive – although, bearing in mind that he was speaking to an audience of motoring journalists, he really missed the opportunity to tell us all that he was looking for a gear change, that he was parking the problem, or that previous management had been asleep at the wheel. But overused car metaphors come later in this book (we'll get to them, don't worry): today I'm thinking about his decision to 'go forward', rather than in any other direction.

I searched Factiva for the phrase 'going forward we...' I added the 'we' so that the results would omit the literal use of going

Figure 1.3   Catching jargon in the public sector

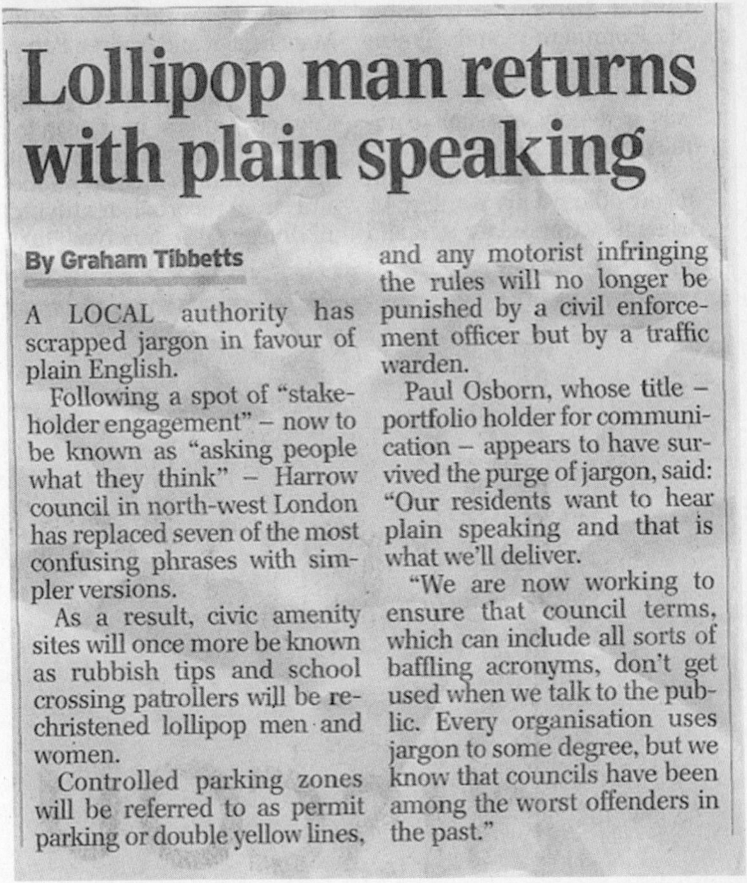

Lollipop man returns with plain speaking

By Graham Tibbetts

A LOCAL authority has scrapped jargon in favour of plain English.

Following a spot of "stakeholder engagement" – now to be known as "asking people what they think" – Harrow council in north-west London has replaced seven of the most confusing phrases with simpler versions.

As a result, civic amenity sites will once more be known as rubbish tips and school crossing patrollers will be re-christened lollipop men and women.

Controlled parking zones will be referred to as permit parking or double yellow lines, and any motorist infringing the rules will no longer be punished by a civil enforcement officer but by a traffic warden.

Paul Osborn, whose title – portfolio holder for communication – appears to have survived the purge of jargon, said: "Our residents want to hear plain speaking and that is what we'll deliver.

"We are now working to ensure that council terms, which can include all sorts of baffling acronyms, don't get used when we talk to the public. Every organisation uses jargon to some degree, but we know that councils have been among the worst offenders in the past."

forward – for example the results would leave out descriptions of footballers going forward on the pitch, but capture the waffle of the club's directors going forward at the AGM (Figure 1.4).

It's a regular and sustained increase, even when you break apart the five-year blocks I have used. Between 1980 and 1985 I could find only six uses of the phrase. Happy days.

'Going forward' is hogging the middle lane of what-to-do-next jargon. To show this, I grouped 'going forward we' to its close relative 'moving forward we', as weasel phrases, and compared them to the two non-MBA phrases 'in future we' and 'from now on we'. We get a Phillips Weasel Index for the trend towards going forwardness

Figure 1.4 How often phrases begin with 'Going forward we...'

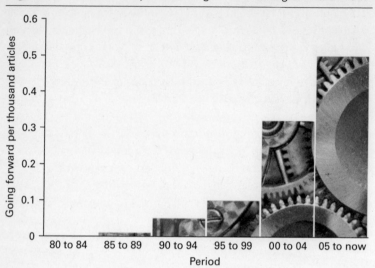

Figure 1.5 Phillips Weasel Index for 'going forward' over 'in the future'

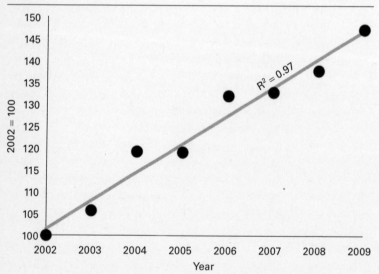

(Figure 1.5). As the line rises, people are substituting 'going/moving forward' for 'in the future'/'from now on'.

Between 2002 and 2009 we became about 50 per cent more likely to do something going forward than to do it either 'in the future' or 'from now on'.

If we really want to be nitpickers – indulge me – then I can try to use my physics A level. Here goes: when we treat time as a fourth dimension it has a property that breadth, depth and height don't have. To use another motoring metaphor, time is a one-way street. In three dimensions you can go back and forth, up and down, left and right. In time you're always heading from the past to the future. You are always going forward because, without Michael J Fox's DeLorean car (more motoring), you can't go back.

So it's a waste of breath when someone tells you that he or she is going to do something 'going forward'. It is redundant, unnecessary, without a function, superfluous, not needed, no longer useful.

You could argue using this logic that 'in the future' or 'from now on' is equally redundant. A good point. On the other hand, only 'going forward' is really, really irritating.

It doesn't stop there, because those of you who are alive to the problems of verbal cliché will be wondering whether weaselly 'on-going' has experienced a similarly graceless rise to pervasiveness. The short answer: yes.

When Reverend Philip Gulley was promoting his book *If the Church Were Christian* in 2009, he complained that the 'ongoingness of the institution is all-important'. You could say his book is about the un-fortunateness of the ongoingness of churchiness.

Even though 'ongoing' has no reason to exist (telling me that there's an ongoing discussion gives me no more information than telling me there's a discussion, for example), it is getting more popular in the press. It is routinely paired with weasel words to make them even more irritating than they were before: imagine that you're about to deal 'a savage redundancies blow to Solihull' (as Fujitsu Telecommunications Europe was accused of doing in the *Solihull News*, 11 December 2011). The first draft of your statement about the problem blames the redundancies on the problems of the economy, but that looks a bit strong. It may be true, it may be accurate, but it is not smooth and reassuring.

Perhaps in the second draft you rename 'the economy' as 'the current economic climate', which sounds more reassuringly weaselly already. You might also downgrade 'problems' to the drippy 'challenges', but you need one more word that will knock the final hard edge off your statement.

Ongoing is that word. Bingo. So a spokesperson for Fujitsu told the confused and probably irritated reporter: 'This has been necessitated by the ongoing challenges of the current economic climate and

Figure 1.6 An ongoing increase

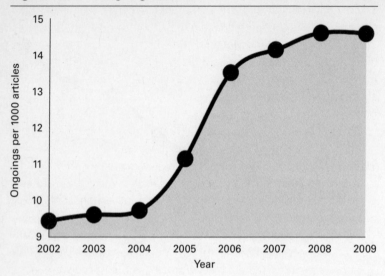

the resultant requirement for Fujitsu Telecommunications Europe to scale its operations in line with anticipated business volumes and mix.'[3]

With a weasel word as useful as 'ongoing', it's hardly surprising that it is catching on outside Solihull's telecommunications industry too (Figure 1.6).

But the real growth is found in pairing ongoing with words like challenge, as in the Solihull redundancies example on page 13. The phrase has increased in frequency by a factor of four since 2002 (Figure 1.7).

Or in turning 'issues' into 'ongoing issues', a phrase that is now five times as common as it was eight years ago (Figure 1.8).

There's hardly a weasel word that you don't find paired with ongoing. Ongoing is the Cliff Richard of weasel words: on its own, irritating yet pointless; in a duet, borderline dangerous.

Giving your all (plus o.8 per cent)

Sporting commentators and their interviewees have arguably had as much influence on the way we talk in the office as a hundred business gurus. The phraseology coined by sweaty men, squeezing Lucozade Sport into the corners of their mouths while someone pokes

Figure 1.7   'Ongoing challenges' in the UK

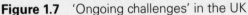

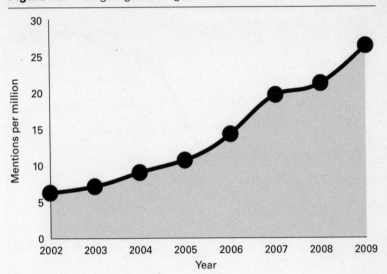

Figure 1.8   'Ongoing issues' in the UK

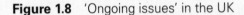

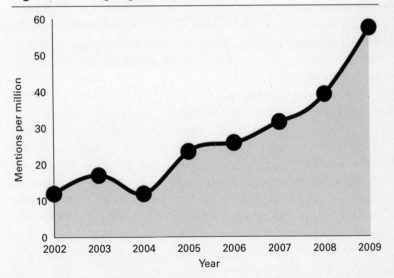

a microphone in their faces and asks idiotic questions, can achieve a certain Zen brilliance of meaninglessness. Business metaphors are often more complex, and look better on the page of a book than on YouTube.

Table 1.1 Business metaphors

Business	Football
Big Hairy Audacious Goal[1]	Big Ask
Six-sigma quality methodologies	Keeping it tight at the back
Kaizen continuous improvement	Take each match as it comes
Black Swan events	It's a funny old game
Compelling value proposition	The team's good on paper
In negative territory	All to play for
Volatility in demand	A game of two halves
Holistic end-to-end approach	Total football
Headhunted	Tapped up

[1] Popularised in the business book *Good to Great*: **http://www.jimcollins.com/**

Both are completely impenetrable unless you're interested in the subject. For example, see Table 1.1. It's arguable who won at the end of the day. There are no easy games at this level. Both sides ran their socks off.

But one area in which I thought sport was innovating was in the redefinition of maximum effort, which for far too long has languished at 100 per cent. I was wrong. Developing economies have discovered that 100 per cent need not be the limit, while sportspeople are even worse than politicians.

I searched for stories where people claimed to give certain percentages (or % or per cent) of effort to find how hard we have been trying in the past few years. I examined a spread from 'give 120 per cent' down to 'give 80 per cent' on the assumption that anyone claiming to give higher or lower percentages is either a fantasist or lazy enough to ignore.

Ideally, sport tells us that any organisation with its name on the cup this year will have a cadre of capable people who tell you they are giving 110 and 120 per cent. Imagine if we let the 100 percenters carry on as before, then we pair each person who claims to give 120 per cent with someone who wants to give 80 per cent, each person

Figure 1.9   Talk Normal effort index, 2009

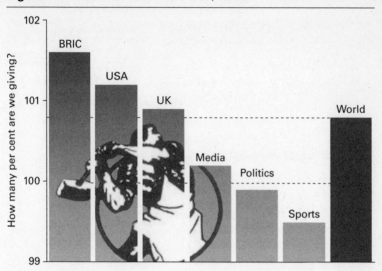

giving 110 with a 90-percenter, and so on. By finding the average I'm effectively measuring who is left over after we do this.

Note that I assume that someone claiming to give 110 per cent is as likely to fulfil that promise as someone who claims to give 90 per cent. This is obviously problematic from a strictly statistical point of view, because it's what statisticians call 'impossible'. So that's problematic also in the sense of 'not true'. But I don't make up the numbers, I just report them.

We need our hyperbolic elites to balance out those who shamelessly give 90 or 80 per cent and aren't scared to tell the press about it. In normal times a society can celebrate both over- and under-achievers, and so will score a solid 100 per cent. Yet, in times of crisis, perhaps more than 100 per cent effort is required – which is why I looked at the statistics for 2009. We're averaging 100.8 globally, so that's all right (Figure 1.9).

I conclude:

1   We're doing better than we used to. At least, we're saying that we're doing better. The global effort mean for the noughties was about 96 per cent.

2   The BRIC (Brazil, Russia, India, China) countries say they're trying harder than we are. Anyone who has ever spent a

couple of hours in the presence of an Indian company manager, watched all those drummers at the opening ceremony of the Beijing Olympics, or looked to see where all your spam comes from will believe this.

3   The UK and the United States are above average. Our economies are dead in the water and we're basically owned by China, but the index shows that we keep telling people that we're trying, which is endearing.

4   Journalists claim to work harder than politicians. But I'm sure politicians are also claiming another couple of per cent in their expenses – not least because they score less than 100 per cent.

Surprisingly, sportspeople are below-average hyperbolists. An odd result considering the number of high-profile bulls***ters who work in the business. The low score is maybe because, even if they insist they're giving 120 per cent, they're giving it twice a week for an hour and a half (though I'm not sure how this would be reflected in the data). Or it might just be that cricket, a game where it's not polite to try too hard and which is the only sport deliberately scheduled around sit-down meals, drags the average down.

So good news: If your peer group wants to top the Talk Normal effort chart next year all you need to do is let the press know that you consistently give 101.7 per cent. You'll be top of my pile for exaggeration, if not for quotability.

Significant: a word I despise

PRINCETON, N.J. – Dataram Corporation [NASDAQ: DRAM]

Capitalising on its 42 year history of delivering meaningful operational improvements and measurable total cost of ownership reductions to an impressive list of financial service customers, today Dataram formally announced the formation of its Financial Services Practice. The newly formed practice will provide unique insight into the most memory-intensive and performance-driven applications within the financial services industry. Dataram memory solutions have a track record of delivering significant performance and optimisation improvements in critical applications, such as, Market Analytics, Real-Time Securities Trading, Trade Processing, Data Mining, High Volume

Transaction Processing, Trade Execution and Settlement, and Market Risk Calculations.

Bruce Magath, Dataram's VP of Marketing and Strategy stated, 'Our memory specialists are highly skilled in deploying the most reliable memory solutions that result in substantial performance improvements...'

From 'Dataram Launches Financial Services Group', *Business Wire*, Sept 15, 2009[4]

Ah! The irony. Dataram Corporation's recent press release about measurable, yes measurable, performance contains exactly two numbers. The first one is the information that Dataram Corp was founded 42 years ago. The second is that it was founded in 1967. So, to be strict, the press release has one number, expressed in two different ways.

Trying to get useful information from this release, as with so many c**ppy self-congratulatory corporate web pages and marketing-driven white papers, is like banging your head against a giant marshmallow. It is vague wherever the precision of which Dataram boasts would be helpful. None of the many extravagant claims in the press release can be usefully understood: the company just speaks well of itself for a few hundred words. It describes operational improvements as 'meaningful', insight as 'unique', its applications as 'performance-driven', the performance itself as 'significant', its specialists as 'highly skilled' (as opposed to all those generalist specialists out there). The result is a 'substantial' performance improvement. It is, we read, a 'tremendous opportunity' because performance (again) is 'high' and the customer's cost of ownership is 'substantially lower'.

Pop quiz: how much lower is 'substantially' lower? Is 'significant' 10 per cent or 80 per cent? What sorts of improvements are 'meaningful' on Dataram's planet?

I have no idea what Dataram is doing here, or has been doing for 42 years, or how well it does it. I could read this tripe for 20 years (which sort of sums up my career so far) and still I'd have no idea.

If there's one tip I could give to anyone who has to churn out this vague optimism, which the rest of us have to read, it's to cut out these weasel words. You're probably going to ignore me, because they're too tempting. 'Significant' and 'substantial' look like they're telling us something, but they aren't. They're useful for people who have a deadline but no clear idea what they're writing about; or people who know the numbers, don't want to tell us what they are,

Figure 1.10 Evidently many things are significant or unique

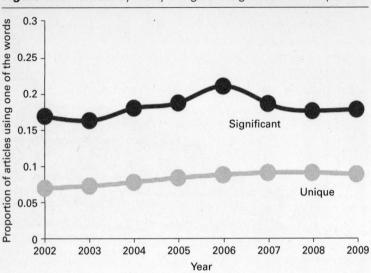

but want to waste our time anyway because that's what they're paid to do. Often they are paid by the word, so chucking in a 'substantial' here and there is basically free money.

On Factiva's database of press releases there's no clear trend upward or downward in the use of any of the non-words that Dataram employed to such non-effect. That would be too much to expect. Non-words have nowhere to live; so they just lie around in documents year after year, pretending to tell us something. For example, look at the graph of the use of 'significant' and 'unique' since 2002 (Figure 1.10).

Nothing much to see there unless, of course, you are concerned that 1 in 12 press releases in the last eight years claims that something is 'unique'. This seems to be setting the bar low for one-of-a-kindness. Remember, 'unique' means there is nothing else like it in the universe: not that it's a bit unusual.

There is, though, a worrying trend in the data. Since 2002 the frequency of press releases with just one of these annoying non-words remains roughly constant; but in 2009 you were three times as likely to find a release that claims all four of our meaningless words – that something is simultaneously 'significant' and 'substantial' and 'meaningful' and 'unique' (Figure 1.11).

Figure 1.11 So throw them all in together

This isn't just a problem of people who make obscure measurement widgets. Non-words are banding together to destroy our ability to think clearly. It's literally a vague threat. Dataram's press release is just one example of the wider problem that meaninglessness is becoming more concentrated, if such a thing is possible.

Say what you mean, mean what you say

Between the ages of 11 and 18 I grew up in Yorkshire which, for non-Yorkies, was a strange and frightening place. People kept telling you what they thought. Years later, I'm starting to appreciate what they were getting at, although that doesn't apply to Mr Parsons, my PE teacher.

Politeness has its uses. It civilises both the person speaking and the person being spoken to. It can coat the message in a non-threatening sauce, which means we listen to what's being said, rather than simply reacting to it. It can convey empathy with our disappointment or fear.

But not always. The word that did most to drive me to create Talk Normal is a simple one: 'issue'. Don't worry, there are much longer words later. This one shows, in my opinion, what's wrong with our jargon culture.

It doesn't seem like jargon. We know more or less what an 'issue' is. It's a conflict, or an unresolved... problem. Often it's a problem. In fact, increasingly it is used to redefine a problem, because 'problem' has become a Yorkshire sort of word: confrontational, signifying possible failure and the need for action. By comparison, an issue implies a bump on the road to success, the sort of thing that can be flattened out if we have a meeting, or just get to know each other a little better.

Around 10 years ago I was asked to train the CEO of a company to speak to the press, because he was doing interviews which they were refusing to print. It wasn't hard to understand why: he never stopped selling. His family must have been exhausted. He didn't invite you into his office; he sold you the benefits of being in his office. He didn't offer a biscuit; he positioned biscuit consumption as a win–win proposition which developed a beneficial partnership.

His company was obviously not so proficient, because it was losing money, had rotten products and customers who were complaining. These were, I said, urgent problems.

'They're not problems', he said. 'I prefer to call them "issues".'
He smiled, as if this made things better.
'You can't call a problem an "issue" to make it go away', I said.
He thought about this.
'You're absolutely right', he said. 'I call it an opportunity!'
Customers probably didn't agree.

It's no longer called a spade

I liked the advertisement shown in Figure 1.12, which I saw on a billboard at London Waterloo station in 2010. Usually advertising irritates me, but this billboard was right on my metaphorical platform.

I thought it would be worth testing whether spades really are being called spades at the moment, so I did a Phillips Weasel Index[5] search using the whole world's published articles about everything since 2003. I compared the number of articles mentioning the word 'spade' with the number that use any of the synonyms for spade listed by Thesaurus.com. It's bad news for Talknormalisers: it suggests you are about twice as likely to find someone literally not

Figure 1.12   It's no longer called a spade

Figure 1.13   PWI for [not spade] / [spade]

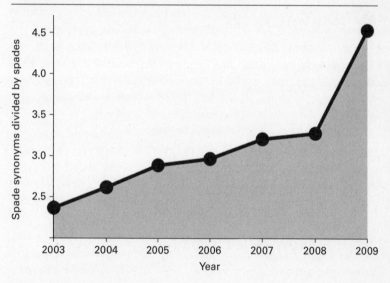

calling a spade a spade as you were six years ago (Figure 1.13). For garden centre managers, driven insane that customers now take so long to ask for the product they want, this is – wait for it – ground-breaking research.

The incomprehensibility of jargon is a much more serious point. You can turn off the radio if Radio Five Live ever invites me back, without missing anything at all. Like most communication, it's merely passing time. There are, however, important parts of our lives in which it is completely and unavoidably vital to know what's being said. Anyone who has ever stared blankly at a book-length form to apply, for example, for a UK residence visa will have passed through irritation and boredom quickly, and entered a state of mild panic at questions so convoluted that it's impossible to work out what the government wants to know.

My point is that jargon isn't always just an annoyance. It's also used for social control. The person using words that you don't understand to explain something that you need to know has power over you. You are on the outside, he or she is on the inside, speaking the insider's language.

It's why we are not going to get very far along the path to Talknormalism until we admit to ourselves that, often, we like jargon because it makes us feel special. How pathetic is that?

My issue with Issues

Just as the US government rebranded the 'War on Terror' as 'The Fight for a Better World' in 2005, so many of us have abandoned the real, truthful yet uncomfortable word 'problem', and substituted the blandly depressing 'issue' instead. It's the worst type of weasel word.

Around 1988 the word 'issue' popped up about as often as the word 'problem', which is not surprising – there are many legitimate uses of the word. But like a linguistic grey squirrel, 'issue' has been quietly taking over. Figure 1.14 shows a graph of the number of times, in UK-based corporate, industry and economics news sources, that the words 'problem' and 'issue' occur every 1,000 articles.

The sample size is getting on for a million articles a year, so it's pretty reliable. In case you're looking at the graph and thinking 'the curves aren't that steep', I have another one of my Phillips Weasel Indices (Figure 1.15). Remember, as the curve goes up, that's more issues compared to problems.

As you can see, in 10 years the ratio has more than doubled. There are now almost three and a half issues per problem. Twenty years ago, the issue/problem PWI was 1.18 – slightly more than one issue per problem. And this is in magazines and newspapers, where people are employed specifically to delete this type of language abuse. In everyday language, I'm guessing the PWI is much higher.

Figure 1.14   How often, in UK-based corporate, industry and economics news sources, the words 'problem' and 'issue' occur in every 1,000 articles

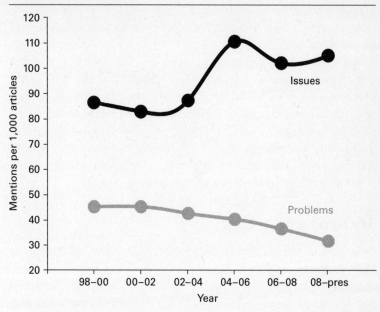

There are two possible explanations relevant to us:

1   Perhaps there are more issues now, and fewer problems. No, I'm not buying that either.

2   Perhaps we are more interested in writing about our issues now, and less interested in our problems? There's no evidence for that in the subject matter: we've never been more obsessed with the 'problems' of doing business.

I think what's occurring is a stealthy rebranding: the word 'problem' has become too emotionally loaded to be uttered in polite company in case we think bad things about the companies responsible. So software bugs are now issues rather than problems, even if they stop our computers working and ruin our day.

Or, for my CEO, the bug is an opportunity. He was in the software business, and the only opportunity a broken computer gives you is the opportunity to wait for tech support to call back.

Figure 1.15 Issues divided by problems

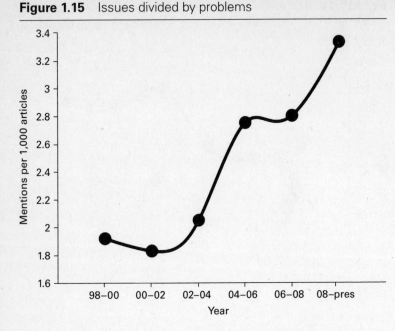

We now have 'performance issues' with staff who fall asleep on their keyboard, or 'brand issues' with companies that nobody likes, or, worst of all, 'balance sheet issues', as described by Lehman Brothers, shortly before it ceased to be Lehman Brothers. At least they didn't call it a 'balance sheet opportunity', though I bet someone suggested it.

Rule of thumb on issues: it doesn't matter whether your company admits to balance sheet issues or problems, it still might be time to send out your CV.

Issues: a postscript

Opposition to my Yorkshirisation of 'issue' back to the word 'problem' runs deep. Specifically, many of the people I've trained don't like it because other people in the company they work for will complain when it makes them look bad. I'd counter that you already look bad to the people who matter: the people who have the problem.[6]

But after I wrote about issues, someone showed me an article from the *Boston Globe*'s 'The Word' column in which author Jan

Freeman snarkily dismisses a complaint from Mr GB that people are using the word 'issue' more often than before.

She wrote:

> Mr. B. is a victim of the **Frequency Illusion**, to use the term coined by linguist Arnold Zwicky. He's listening for issues, so he hears the word often, and imagines that it's everywhere. In fact, in the specific usage he objects to – having issues instead of having problems – the problems version is still way, way ahead of issues.

Her evidence: she did a Google search for each term. On this basis she dismissed the idea that we might be uncomfortable describing problems honestly.

You're wrong, Jan Freeman! I know they don't pay much for columns these days, but an analysis that took more than 30 seconds on a search engine would have shown that this is probably not a Zwickian illusion at all. Which makes her snobby putdown that 'Mr. B.'s analysis is more puzzling than his failure to check the facts' doubly unfortunate.

But it's her conclusion that I found depressing: '...issues aren't always problems; they are also anxieties, conflicts, and disagreements. And if the word is meant to make those conflicts sound less dire, isn't that a good thing? After all, anyone who'd rather have problems than issues is welcome to them.'

I'd rather have been an astronaut than a journalist but, if I started turning up for interviews in a space suit, people might point out that I wasn't facing up to the reality of my situation. It's the same thing: when we can't utter the word 'problem' at work in case it makes us unhappy, we're living a destructive fantasy.

The problem of word obesity

That's my own jargon: word obesity[7] is the process by which we take small words and replace them with larger words. We then take the larger words, and expand them. We then start to substitute the little words for obese ones without thinking. Then we pop extra words into our sentences as well, just like having a Mars bar to tide us over until dinner.

The result: a form of written language in which formal, Latin-derived words obscure the meaning, and where nothing that's written in three pages couldn't be better expressed in one. Why do we do this? Again, word has spread that it's what we need to do to sound flash.

Note also that weasel words aren't always short. Some are so long as to be almost unpronounceable.

We're also unconstrained. When printing was expensive and boring, when letters were handwritten and typing was done by typists, there was an incentive to be brief. Now, we can keep typing until we're bored of transcribing the sound of our own voice. Anecdotal evidence suggests that we take a long time to get bored.

There's also a tiresome trend to add redundant syllables: we will see how that has created growth in the word 'operate' in a second. But ask yourself: when did preparing become 'pre-preparing'? When was planning first thought of as 'pre-planning?' Either some people in the office are preparing to prepare, or just adding a bit at the front to emphasise how pro-proactive they are.

Remember: when you fail to pre-prepare, you prepare to prepare to fail.

I feel so utilised

Even the simplest words get bloated when we're busy trying to sound clever. Here's an example: you don't get much simpler or more effective than the verb 'to use'. It's a word we use (see) all the time, especially at home. But when we leave for work we take easy-to-understand 'use' and stick an extra two syllables in it, and it becomes conference-room-hell-word 'utilise'.

And it's getting much worse, very quickly. Look at the Phillips Weasel Index of the relative frequency of use and utilise (I included utilize, for our international readers) from 2002 to the end of 2009 (Figure 1.16): the higher the graph goes, the more we are substituting 'use' out of the language for 'utilise' – a word that takes us longer to say and type, but we think it makes us sound like we've done an MBA.

As you can see, that's a rise of more than 60 per cent in seven years. This PWI increase is consistent across technology, business, software, telecoms and media. The exception is for press releases, where there has been no rise in the PWI since 2002. Way to go, press release writers!

Figure 1.16   Phillips Weasel Index for utilise (-ize) / use (2002 = 1)

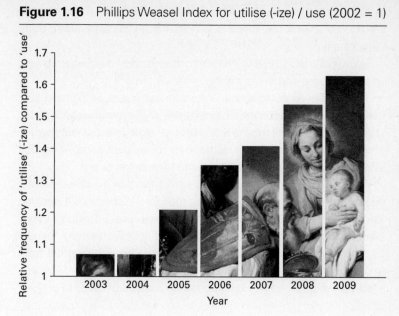

Actually, it just shows that you started writing badly earlier than the rest of us, and you continue to outperform. In 2002 you were about three-and-half-times as likely as a journalist to stick 'utilise' instead of 'use' in your paragraph in a misguided attempt to make your client sound clever, and now it's down to a factor of about 2.3.

Rule of thumb: we all speak in different ways to different groups. Personally, I catch myself adopting a ridiculous mockney accent when talking to taxi drivers, I don't know why. But we can train ourselves to be better, to talk to the people at work in the same way we talk at home. On the other hand, if you say to your kids 'which one of you utilised the last pint of milk?' then your training needs are more fundamental.

A big word problem

The journalist Justin Webb from Radio 4's *Today* programme in September 2010 tweeted that: 'Can't talk simple this am: pay becomes renumeration and softness emollience. Coffee please.'

Several people tweeted while he was at the coffee machine to tell him that the word he was looking for was remuneration (the 'm' before the 'n'), but I sympathise with Justin. I didn't realise that renumeration meant 'counting something again', and not 'earned money', until I was about 30 years old.

I still have trouble saying and typing the word. More embarrassing, I have similar problems with the word laboratory. It's a good job I never worked for the chemistry press, or my peers would have split their sides when I asked questions at press conferences.

Justin and I are not alone with this remun/renum mix-up: journalists have used renumeration when they mean remuneration around 100 times a year for the past 10 years (you have no idea how long this blog is taking me to type). On 23 August 2010 *Chemical Week* made the same error. Ha! Who's laughing now, chemists? Wearing your white coats, reading your trade paper in your labra-, lobaro-, your places of work.

If you suffer because you can't say or spell remuneration, I don't care, because – unlike nucular – it's a weasel word that doesn't need our respect. It's a classic case of word obesity. Take Justin's advice and say 'pay' instead: problem solved. Everyone understands what you mean and you don't sound pompous. Both my 1965 edition of *Fowler's Modern English Usage* (I write as if I have copies from other years) and Harold Evans' *Essential English for Journalists* agree.

You know what's next: I made a Phillips Weasel Index of the relative frequency of 'remuneration' against 'pay' (both in articles also containing the word 'job') from 2001 to 2009. The data is from articles published in North America and Europe (Figure 1.17).

The complicated word is twice as frequent as it was in 2001, but 'pay' is almost unchanged in frequency. Most of the growth in use of renumer-, remuren-, that word has happened since 2007. Perhaps it is because we are rarely more than a day away from a story about what bankers are banking for themselves, and 'pay' doesn't seem grand enough for their piles of unearned income and bonuses.

Maybe the word we use to describe income should have at least as many letters as the income has digits, which means that only cleaners without visas and bloggers earn 'pay' these days.

What about the rest of us? For Talknormalisers who want to feel special about pay, but like me can't pronounce the obese version, I'd suggest describing it as 'compensation'. It's a bit pompous, but I like it because it sounds like they gave us the cash out of sympathy, which matches the experience of work that most of us have.

Figure 1.17 Don't pay me, remunerate me.
Relative frequency of words, 2001–09

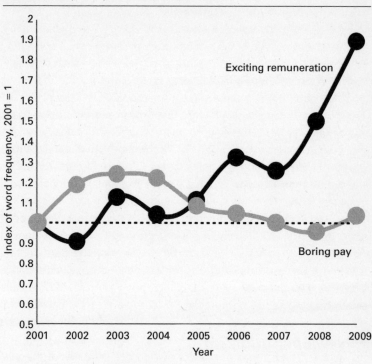

The cure: try reading it to yourself

In the preface to *The God Delusion*, Richard Dawkins describes how he refines his writing by asking his wife, the actor Lalla Ward, to read his words aloud to him 'so I could apprehend very directly how it might seem to a reader other than myself... I recommend the technique to other authors, but I must warn that for best results the reader must be a professional actor, with voice and ear sensitively tuned to the music of language', he says.

You'd have to have a heart of stone not to see the amusement value of Professor Dawkins – who I think is a terrific writer – listening to his wife declaim all 420 pages of his book, maybe from a little lectern in his front room. And she did the whole book twice, he explains. She must love him very much.

Dawkins' advice to marry an actor so that he or she can read your work to you might seem impractical, especially to your current spouse, but Dawkins has a point – which his prose reinforces. You might disagree with his concept of a godless universe, but if you have read *The God Delusion* you wouldn't say that he expresses himself with anything less than complete clarity. You can disagree with him because you know exactly what he's thinking.

We're accustomed to writing far more than telling. Many of us will have carefully written a presentation, printed it out, got to the front of the room, and realised that it's almost unreadable. In trying to make ourselves sound good, we make ourselves sound bad: using long, clause-filled sentences, multiple trains of thought, and – most of all – obese words. Even if we're writing something as simple as an e-mail, the other person will be reading it for the first time, a voice in their heads making sense of what you wrote.

Or, perhaps, realising it is nonsense. Some public figures are extremely good at trotting out long strings of syllables. When we try to do the same, it's usually embarrassing. Even if they manage to make it work, there's a limit to how far we can stretch a word before we lose all sense of meaning. People who have this habit should be forced to read out their work, preferably to Richard Dawkins when he's in a bad mood. That'll cure them.

Polysyllabilisationism

I was struck recently by a politician who stated that his country was ready to 'operationalise' a strategy, which obviously has consequences. Quite apart from anything else, a civil servant now has to draw up an operationalisation plan.

If civil servants are paid by the syllable, I can see the point in this. Otherwise, I'd like to helpfully point out – in the interests of public sector efficiency – that an operationalisation plan can also be described as 'a plan'.

You can just keep stretching a word like 'operate', but that doesn't mean it is a good idea to do so. I took this word as a base to see how well we're doing at stuffing it with extra syllables. Not surprisingly, useful extensions like 'operation' and 'operational' have more or less exactly the same long-term relative frequency, though 'operational' is growing in frequency, maybe because it sounds macho (Figure 1.18).

Not much to see there. But let's add the politician's word that started all this: 'operationalise' (Figure 1.19). To catch all the examples, I spelt it using both the -ise and -ize forms. This extension is getting

Figure 1.18 The path to operationalisationism

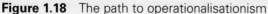
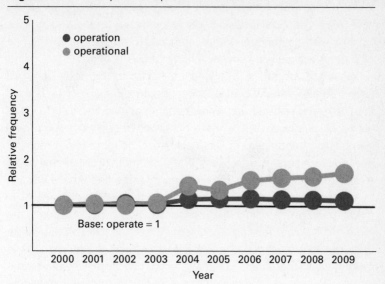

Figure 1.19 The path to operationalisationism

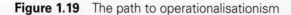
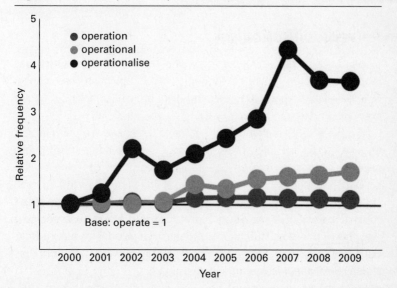

much more popular. I'm guessing it is crowding out the phrase that you would use if you were talking, 'put into operation', which doesn't make you sound important at all.

Figure 1.20 The path to operationalisationism

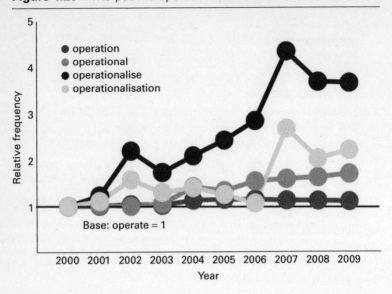

I wondered if anyone had the nerve to commit a word like operation-alisation to print and, I kid you not, there were almost 400 examples of it in 2009 alone (Figure 1.20).

It's becoming more popular, but not gaining in popularity as fast as 'operationalise'. I think that's for two reasons:

1 From the examples I could be bothered to read, there's just no point to it; which is a disadvantage even for clever-sounding words.

2 It's just as hard to type as it is to say.

Two good reasons to stop right here, but you know we can't do that. On 29 October 2009, in the transcript of a Zygo Corporation earnings conference call, the world was introduced to the first-ever recorded example of the word 'operationalisational' in a business context. Nine syllables! I can't help feeling that future historians will date some kind of decline from this moment, lamenting that a once great culture choked to death by gorging itself on its own syllables.

Deceived by weasels

Our journey through weasel world has led from obscure technical terms, through the words that make us feel important, to the obese words we put into documents when we can't think of something to say. But we reach the end with the reminder of where we started: that for all the amusement that it causes, this type of language is used by cynical people to confuse you into believing that something is being said, when it really isn't.

We'll deal in more detail with marketing junk later, but examine, for the moment, the 'Customer Charter' that NatWest Bank is using to convince us that it has binding 'commitments' to our welfare.

We care, somewhat

Here are some of the commitments:

> 'We will aim to serve the majority of customers within 5 minutes in our branches.'
> 'We will continue to be a responsible lender and are committed to finding new ways to help.'
> 'We will actively seek your thoughts and suggestions on how we can become more helpful.'

What does the first one mean? On first glance, that staff will serve you within five minutes. That's terrific; I usually wait at least 10 minutes in my local branch, where I always seem to be paying in a cheque just behind someone who's paying in the month's takings from an amusement arcade. But it doesn't say that. The majority get served within five minutes: so as long as 51 per cent of customers get served in this time, the commitment's good. It doesn't mean you will be in the 51 per cent.

And there's a further level of meaninglessness: note that it's a commitment to 'aim' to do this. When you take an oath in court, you don't swear to aim to tell the truth, the whole truth and nothing but the truth the majority of the time. A commitment to 'aim to' do something is nothing more than a vague, weasely 'aim'. It's no longer a 'commitment', because now trying a bit and failing has become as good as trying a lot and succeeding.

The business is committed to finding new ways to lend money. Seeing as lending money is its business (this is a bank), this is a commitment, in the same way that 'I commit to writing words just as long as I'm paid to do that' is a commitment. NatWest will also commit to seek your thoughts, but doesn't commit to acting on them. As a commitment, that's merely saying that the staff won't put their fingers in their ears and sing 'la la la' when you complain; but they're not committing to write down what you said afterwards either.

The commitments sound committed, but they are cleverly crafted to sound that way to busy people who are thinking about other things – which is a good description of everyone in a bank queue. Throughout this chapter, the emptiness of people who wish to sound clever has been a recurring theme. When people do it because they want to be appreciated, it's understandable, because we all do it. When they do it to convince us to believe they are promising something that they don't promise at all, we're being manipulated for profit.

It's too easy: in this case, we're the pathetic ones.

For those of you who read political manifestos, this downgrading of commitment is commonplace. It continues after a manifesto becomes policy, and especially after the policy translates to action. NatWest is far from the worst offender.

Ann McElvoy, policy editor at *The Economist*, points out that Prime Minister David Cameron's apparent promise in 2010 not to tinker with the National Health Service (NHS) was nothing of the sort:

> Cameron said his 'priority' was the NHS. It's a very clever phrase when you think about it because 'priority' sounds lovely and warm, but it doesn't tell you what you intend to do with it. It could mean the NHS is a priority because you are trying to safeguard it. It could mean your priority is to shake it up. It turns out he meant the latter.

Weasel words can have consequences for your health: the price of Talknormalism is eternal vigilance.

Whatever doesn't work

In 2009, the Marist Institute in New York announced that Americans find 'whatever' to be the most irritating word in the language. In their research it beat my particular favourite, 'at the end of the day', and left 'going forward' in the dust.

Without defending 'whatever' as a generic response used by our youth, I'd point out that people in suits often do the same thing. They use fancy language and have PR consultants to help them pretend it's something else.

I once attended a gala dinner after which I would be allowed to ask Bill Gates, when he was the world's richest man and the boss of Microsoft, a single question. I planned it carefully. I phrased it so that there was no easy answer. The others at the dinner were customers who could be relied on to offer softball questions. I was determined to be different.

I was handed the microphone. Triumphantly, I asked my question. 'That's not the question you should be asking about this subject,' Gates replied, 'what you should be asking is...' I looked for the microphone. It had gone, as had my opportunity.

I'm not saying that every question needs an answer. There are plenty of good reasons for not commenting. There might be legal restrictions, or you might need to keep something secret until a particular day for commercial reasons. That's your business, I'm not your boss. But what really irks me is the number of 'no comment' answers that we get from those in power, either when there's a clear public interest to be served or a clear business reason to comment – because, for example, it shows respect for angry customers.

Politicians call it 'bridging':

They say 'That's a good question'.
They 'bridge' to another subject.
They talk about that instead.

I bristle when someone tells me I've asked a good question, because I know it's not going to get an answer.

More people are copying the politicians and chief executives they hear on the radio and TV. In my experience it goes like this:

SPOKESPERSON: While this type of tittle-tattle may be of interest to a small group of journalists back in the real world, what we should be talking about are the enormous strides that we have made this year in delivering a world-class inkjet printer cartridge replacement service under enormous and frankly unreasonable pressure from people like yourselves.

ME: So you're not going to tell me your job title then?

It's the business equivalent of 'whatever'. Perhaps if more spokes-people just started saying, 'yeah, like, whatever' instead of their elaborate excuses not to communicate, the world would be a more honest place. And it would open up new opportunities in corporate communications for feral teenagers, where their demographic is scandalously under-represented.

Dr Peter Bull, a psychologist from York University, has identified 35 different ways that politicians use to avoid answering a question. Journalist Daniel Finkelstein recalls the story that the politician Dr David Owen once fell asleep on TV. The interviewer asked what he thought of the point that political rival Geoffrey Howe had just made. Owen woke up and said: 'That's not the real issue in this election.' He changed the subject, and carried on. Now that's whateverism of the highest order. Just please don't copy it.

Talknormalise me

It's hard to stop trying to sound clever: it's like a jargon diet. We can be our own conscience, but there are two ways we can make progress. First, we shouldn't follow leaders – at least, not until I'm one. Second, we need to point out the faults we see. Neither is the blueprint for advancement in our careers, but let me explain why they are so important.

The Wombat diversion

We sneakily admire politicians while we affect to despise them. They go on the TV or the radio and say the most outrageous things with a straight face. Amazing.

This is not Talking Normal. Do not do this at home.

One of the tactics employed is the Wombat Diversion: saying something along the lines of the 'Look! A Giant Wombat is attacking parliament!' when asked a different question.

There are variants. If you engage in debate on the internet, you will be aware of the straw man, also learnt from the political arena: someone misrepresents your argument, demonstrates that his misrepresentation is ridiculous, and uses that to argue against you. For example: you're trying to argue that Talk Normal is a force for good in the world with someone we will call 'Weird troll' – because we can play their game too.

> **YOU:**   I think Talk Normal is terrific. That guy could really teach trolls how to argue on the internet, and the world would be a better place.
>
> **WEIRD TROLL:**   But it just says all communication is rubbish. That's stupid. I read a book last year and it was brilliant, and the TV show where people get knocked into the water by a big foam hammer is excellent, so he must be an idiot.

Of course it's not usually giant furry critters that get the blame when politicians are misdirecting; single parents and economic migrants are much more compelling as diversions from their own faults. Also, pointing at your competition and saying 'Look at them! They're just as bad as we are', then doing a runner, is considered a good way to change the story.

In the lead-up to the 2010 general election, journalists noticed this distraction technique in overdrive in the UK government. All people wanted to talk about was when public spending would be cut. We now know that using the word 'cut' was considered so damaging that it was ruled out, and so politicians would fire back that 'It's more important to talk about the investments we are making...', and so on. Hard to believe people want to copy this, but that's the world we made for ourselves. It was like a party game: he can't say it, you have to try to make him say it, he will try to distract you. A tedious party game at that, and one that was based entirely on their own futile lust for influence.

As this was going on, I measured the number of articles discussing the Labour party and spending cuts (Figure 1.21). In a pleasurable outbreak of Talknormalism, more and more of the articles stopped being about the cuts themselves, but about how the politicians refused to talk about those cuts. Manipulation failed spectacularly: in September 2009, a quarter of all political articles about Labour mentioned the 'C' word.

It's my theory that Wombat Diversions – not just for politicians, but for anyone in power – are becoming less effective, but only if we call them out.

We are more comfortable than our parents were with the idea of leaders as liars and cheats who are cynically manipulating us based

Figure 1.21   Labour stories about cuts, 2009–10

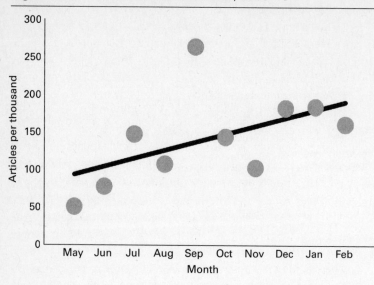

on little more than their lust for wealth and glory. Maybe 'comfortable' isn't quite the word, but you see what I mean. And so, at that point, we stop looking for what they are saying, and start looking for what they are not saying, and discuss that instead. The longer they keep not saying it, the harder we look.

Second, it's much easier to spot evasion and misdirection when you can Google it afterwards. A Wombat Diversion might keep the story off the front pages in the short term, but thanks to internet reporting there are an unlimited number of other pages where it can incubate.

A sad consequence of this is that, when mutant Wombats really do attack the Mother of Parliaments, it will take us by surprise. 'Why didn't the powers that be warn us?' we will ask as giant furballs chomp their way through the House of Lords.

Talk Normal's debt to Katie Price's breasts

So to the most important part of Talknormalism: when you see something you hate, speak out. I can't do this alone.

This is the appropriate time to tell the story of model, author, and TV star Katie Price's decision[8] to acquire larger breasts, my influence on her decision, and how those iconic breasts inspired Talk Normal. I hope they will inspire you too.

Many years ago, Jordan (as she was then) was an up-and-coming young topless model, and I was asked to appear on the same TV programme as her. It was an after-the-pub Friday night show put out by Meridian TV, and my job was to explain how to log in to the internet to watch amateur webcams, empowering a generation of drunk men to scour chatrooms for an internet friend who might take her shirt off after hours of pleading. For some reason the researchers had called the editor of *Guardian Online* for advice on this noble pastime, and the *Guardian* (understandably not wanting to soil itself, but correctly assuming I'd do it for £60 cash plus train fare) suggested me.

Jordan had been booked to do some flirty links for the show while wearing tiny clothes. It's a good job they didn't get our scripts mixed up, though she could probably have done a decent job with mine.

Anyway, someone had broken something on the set, so we all sat in the green room for a few hours while men with hammers fixed it. There was a glum US stand-up comedian and a guy who rode muddy motorbikes for a living. Jordan's *Gladiator* boyfriend Ace was there to keep her company while we tucked into the free booze and crisps backstage. Comedy, motorbikes, muscles, partial nudity, chardonnay and modems. That was the 1990s for you. Crazy, crazy days.

And so it came to pass that, after a few glasses, Jordan asked us all her opinion on whether she ought to have a boob job. At that time her breasts were what a certain type of website calls natural, though it wasn't the first adjective that popped into your head when you met her. She was thinking about it, she said, because a newspaper had offered to pay for her breast enhancement on the condition that they got an exclusive right to photograph the results. It seemed like a good offer to her. Ace stared furiously at the Doritos and said 'I always tell Katie she's got quite enough already'.

When it was my turn to speak, I planned to say, 'What are you thinking? You're hardly out of school! The tabloid press will turn you into a human freakshow! You already look like a pencil with two tennis balls sellotaped to it! Are you mad?'

Instead, when she pointed herself at me and said, 'What do you fink? Should I have them done?', I looked at my feet and said, bravely: 'Oh, I dunno.'

I don't know who paid for her boobs in the end, but the next time I saw her in the newspapers she was a much bigger woman. Maybe, in reflective moments, when she contemplates the sadness of being made to eat bugs in the jungle by vengeful reality TV viewers, she thinks, 'Why didn't that bald nerd I met all those years ago in Southampton warn me it would come to this?' I'm sorry, Katie.

It is this failure of nerve that resolved me to do what a blogger should do at all times: to speak truth to power, no matter how many product marketing managers, marketing communications consultants or brand ambassadors I upset. That is why, without Katie Price, we wouldn't have this fragile and precious thing we call Talk Normal.

We all have times when we talk c**p to avoid saying what we know to be true. Next time you are faced with your own Jordan Boob Dilemma (JBD) in your work, don't mumble about challenges and facilitation and win–win scenarios while thinking 'that is a truly terrible idea'.

I ask that we honour Talknormalism by saying what we think when people flout our principles, as I should have done all those years ago.

Notes

1 If you panic at the sight of statistics, don't worry – my graphs are easy to understand.
2 On 7 October 2008, I clipped this from the *Daily Telegraph*, and kept it like a lunatic obsessive.
3 Translation: we're making 140 people redundant.
4 The whole, horrible thing is at http://bit.ly/dataramwaffle.
5 The Phillips Weasel Index crops up many times in this book. It is designed to show the relative frequency of words over time: it's a ratio. On the top a weasel word, or a jargon word, on the bottom the word that the jargon replaces. If the graph goes up, the jargon's catching on. In this case, I tested for all the synonyms-of-spade against 'spade'.
6 There's a school of thought that we can be so dismissive of problems because, to us, the people who have the problems are remote and don't matter, whereas our work colleagues are sitting opposite us and are often friends – and we want to make them happy by systematically downplaying their part in corporate incompetence. Hence 'issues'.

7 Some would say that 'obesity' is like 'issue' – a weasel word that has been popularised to take the negative emotional connotations away from the word 'fatness' by 'medicalising' the condition. Health minister Anne Milton said exactly this in July 2010.

8 First revealed in Talk Normal on 17 December 2009. As yet I have received no requests to take part in a reality show, unlike almost everybody else who has used their acquaintance with Ms Price for publicity purposes, but I live in hope.

2 Office life

Work/life balance

We're not in the office to enjoy ourselves. This is abundantly clear. The Japanese even have a special word for suicide from overwork: they call it *karoshi*. In the year 2000, 33,000 people committed *karoshi*.

If you're thinking of joining them, I understand – up to a point. Obviously I sit at a desk writing books, so my biggest gripes tend to be that my mouse button is sticking, or that someone, who may or may not have been sending messages to her Facebook friends, moved my Anglepoise lamp between 10.21 and 11.43 this morning.

This goes to show that, if you work for long enough, anything can drive you to the borders of insanity.

It doesn't help that we have to put up with all sorts of c**p because we are brainwashed that it's the best way to live. The psychologist Dave Arnott wrote a book called *Corporate Cults* in which he argues that the corporation steals your soul by behaving just like a religious cult: if the definition of a cult is a place with charismatic leadership that inspires devotion and separates you from your community, well that's what your job is trying to do. Even worse, he points out that when *Fortune* magazine publishes its list of best places to work, the criteria (Sense of Purpose, Inspiring Leadership, Knockout Facilities) are basically measuring how good a cult it is.

This begins to explain why so many of us use a weird jargonspeak at work that we'd giggle at when we're at home. If Talknormalism is to succeed, we must build our revolutionary cadre not among the proletariat, but among the product marketing managers, brand specialists and operations executives of the modern workplace.

We must become wise to the techniques by which they seek to sap our will. We must strike back against the documents, meetings and phone calls which hypnotise us with their barely comprehensible jargon; the overbearing sales directors who recognise only the win–win of low-hanging fruit; the ambitious MBA graduate with a hard disk full of pie charts, but nothing coherent to say.

We must storm the gates of marketing (unless you already work there, in which case could you open the gate for us please?), and reject fake happiness, insincere backslapping and tedious hyperbole.

Read the rest of this chapter, and start today. Unless you're not allowed to read books at work, in which case read it tonight and start tomorrow. No later: you're already one day closer to *karoshi*, and we need to nail the people whose language abuse is driving you there.

Emotionally unreachable

The language is constantly changing to match our desires. As our work becomes more remote and programmatic, with fewer face-to-face conversations, we apply the language of emotional yearning and satisfaction to simple day-to-day processes. An example: I'm constantly surprised how often people I speak to in other offices thank me for 'reaching out' to them, when all I've done is ask for some information.

It seemed to borrow from the language of therapy, and is certainly more popular among my US contacts, so maybe I'm just surprised because I'm a bit stuck up. I once had a US boss who told me that my work was 'very British'. I only realised later that she was trying to tell me it was tedious.

I decided to investigate how often we talk about reaching out at each end of our special relationship. The results are shown in Figure 2.1: a graph of how often 'reach out' is mentioned in the news

Figure 2.1 How often 'reach out' is mentioned in the news pages of UK and US magazines and newspapers

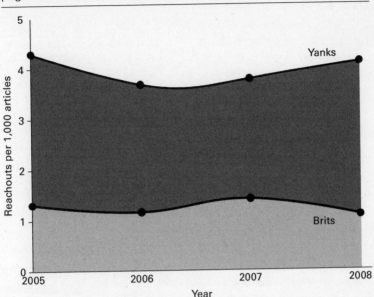

pages of magazines and newspapers in each country. It is clear that British people are saying 'Hey! Don't go there', about the phrase. At least we would, if we knew what that meant too.

Americans are currently about three times as likely to reach out, and when you look deeper into the data, many of the examples in British publications involve grey (gray)-import reaching out: US news articles republished in the UK.

In the UK things are different. We don't like reaching out much now, but back in the 1980s we didn't do it at all: the only mentions were in US-based writing that had been republished. We have never been, it seems, a nation of reach-outers. Look at the graph between 1980 and 2000 (Figure 2.2).

Part of me wants to condemn this, but while I find it faintly ridiculous, I don't think it is a crime against Talknormalism. However, there's something vaguely culty about it to my ear: I'm not reaching out, I'm doing my job.

So maybe Brits aren't swayed by faddy and meaningless psychobabble and so we prefer descriptions of business communication that don't pretend that some emotional need is being satisfied by

Figure 2.2 How often 'reach out' is mentioned in the news pages of UK and US magazines and newspapers (excluding US news articles republished in the UK)

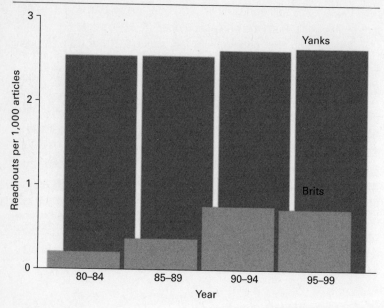

doing our tedious, underpaid jobs. Or maybe we're just snooty and emotionally repressed, a point that I've just reinforced.

Things have changed around here

In our parents' day, offices were places where people got on with things. Communication was for specialists. A couple of times a year, someone from management would tell you something.

That person didn't have a PowerPoint deck, so he or she had to make sure that you understood the words. There were no takeaways or leave-behinds, so you had to get the gist at that moment. Often they were trained to do this.

Our job was not to discuss our job, it was to do it. I recently had a conversation with a manager from Microsoft who wanted to give advice to those of us who were 'about to embark on our collaboration journey'[1] using his software. We've made 'working together' into 'collaboration' because then we need a collaboration strategy, some collaboration systems, and lots of collaboration tools, and they make us feel jolly important.

It gets better, because then we can create concepts like 'cross-functional team collaboration', which is an obese phrase for 'meetings with people from the office next door'. You can't create an Action Plan for meeting with people next door though: either they come to you, or you come to them.

Now we're all telling people things, all the time. When we know what we want to do, we make a plan for doing it, we inform other people who have nothing to do with it, we get suggestions from people who know nothing about it, we examine those suggestions as if they were useful, we document it, we present it to 'stakeholders', and we strategise it. Talking about what we're doing is much more fun and offers less chance of getting caught out, so there's usually no shortage of people to do it.

You might like this approach, in which case there's a huge shelf of management books about how to look impressive while you're doing it on the shelf to your right. If, however, it's making you crazy but you don't know who to blame, read on, I've got some ideas.

Collaboration's dark side

Working together is useful, satisfying and efficient. Working together is frustrating, wastes time and is pointless: I could have done the job in half the time if they would have just let me get on with it.

Type buzzword bingo into Google and any number of sites will pop up which you can use to print off a bingo card. As your manager uses a jargon phrase on your card in a meeting, you can tick it off. It's fun, but does it help? We need a new attitude to meetings.

Problem 1: there are far too many people in them. In his 1975 book *The Mythical Man Month*, IBM manager Fred Brooks described the project to build OS/360, the operating system for one of IBM's giant computers. The computers were huge, but OS/360 had fewer lines of code than Windows 7, or even the operating system for your mobile phone.

On the other hand, the project never seemed to finish. It was the largest software project attempted up to that time, but it was late, and kept getting later. Every time this happened, IBM assigned more people to the project, and the deadlines slipped further behind.

This led to Brooks' Law: adding people to a late project makes it run even later.

The reason: those people need to be briefed, to communicate with people on the project already, to be brought up to speed by those who have experience of the project, and to join meetings. So you're not only wasting time in getting to the point where they can be productive, you're pulling your most valuable people off productive work to do it.

A team of two people has one connection. A team of 10 has 45 connections. Collaboration tends to be a one-way street: once you've added people to the project, it's hard to unadd them. That seems rude, and it's not the way we do things. It might, however, be exactly the way we should do things. The ability to say: we don't need you. The ability to say: let's not discuss this. You do it, then we can discuss what you did.

Problem 2: we think that software makes collaboration better. Not necessarily, but software makes overcommunication easier. An example is the most prolific creator of collaboration software the world has yet seen: Microsoft. Note, I didn't say 'the best'.

An example: Moisshe Lettvin is a software engineer at Google who worked for Microsoft on and off between 1994 and 2006. During that time, one of his jobs was to compile a list of items that would be in one menu in Windows Vista, when he was part of a collaboration called the 'Windows Mobile PC User Experience Team', which was modifying the code from the 'Windows Shell Team', as well as working with the 'kernel Team'. In a blog called 'the Windows Shutdown Crapfest',[2] he detailed how 43 people (903 connections) got involved in a year-long collaboration involving weekly planning meetings and presentations, which went like this:

Approximately every 4 weeks, at our weekly meeting, our PM would say, 'the shell team disagrees with how this looks/feels/works' and/or 'the kernel team has decided to include/not include some functionality which lets us/prevents us from doing this particular thing'. And then in our weekly meeting we'd spent approximately 90 minutes discussing how our feature – er, menu – should look based on this 'new' information. Then at our next weekly meeting we'd spend another 90 minutes arguing about the design, then at the next weekly meeting we'd do the same, and at the *next* weekly meeting we'd agree on something... just in time to get some other missing piece of information from the shell or kernel team, and start the whole process again.

The result: after a year, he had written about 200 lines of code – the work of a couple of hours in the normal run of things.

So my first problem with work is that we collaborate indiscriminately. We involve people out of politeness, rather than because their input is essential. The second is that we talk without a purpose. One company I work with has developed its meeting culture to update progress, when often there has been no progress. The people in the meeting often complain, without a trace of irony, that they haven't had the chance to do anything because they've been in meetings all week. Presumably they leave to the next meeting, where they repeat the same excuse, because they were in a meeting with us.

My second is that we think that collaborating solves our problems. In this case, a problem shared is often a problem doubled – not least because when it's everybody's problem, there's always a reason why it's not yours to solve.

Things reached a particular low point in 2007 in the UK, when the UK Department for Business, Enterprise and Regulatory Reform (BERR) issued its response to the government's Code of Practice on consultation. This document had been compiled by 'stakeholder groups of various government departments', and was the result of 'market research to seek the view of members of the public'. This document[3] is, then, the output of a collaborative consultation on consultations. Which would have meant that the planning meetings at BERR that decided on whether to launch the document were consultations about the consultation on consultations. And so it goes on.

Talknormalism can have a positive effect on two elements of office collaboration in particular: conference calls and presentations.

Conference call etiquette[4]

If there's one step on the collaboration journey I wish I'd never taken, it's the conference call.

I'm doing more conference calls these days, but so is everyone else. It's the perfect activity if you are working from home: your boss knows you are apparently doing something, but it's the sort of activity that needn't interrupt other home-office tasks – such as watching *Homes Under The Hammer*, or playing internet poker.

Another reason that I'm doing more calls is that, for decision makers who don't like to make decisions, it's the answer to every question:

ME: If penguins wore trousers, would they be better off with a belt or braces? They've got no hips, but no shoulders either.

DECISION MAKER: I'll set up a call.

There are informal rules of etiquette for these calls. If you are new to conference calling, the most important thing is to have another activity – such as deleting spam, indulging in ritualised self-harm, or squeezing out quiet tears of rage – that you can perform comfortably at your desk during the call.

I almost finished that paragraph off with '...to avoid disappointment', which is ridiculous. Conference calls are institutionalised disappointment. We tolerate them only because we don't have to look each other in the eyes while we waste each other's lives.

So, for newbies, this is what to expect:

Day minus 2: Marketing Person 1 decides we need a call to discuss the Penguin Pants Project Crisis that you have created. A flurry of e-mails results, during which we establish that there are no mutually acceptable times for the next three months. Eventually Alpha Male 1 sends an irritated e-mail saying that his PA could possibly try to move some things around for him because he's about to get on a flight to Singapore. PA instantly offers six available slots in the next 48 hours. The call is set up for the day after tomorrow.

D –1: Marketing Person 1 sends calendar notification to all announcing that The Bridge Has Been Set Up. It includes dial-in details for a list of 25 countries, not including the one you are in – but including Slovakia and Norway, where your company doesn't have offices.

Day zero: Emails from three people asking if our call is still going ahead, because if not they have another call that's quite important, but don't worry they'll cancel the other call, even though it's quite important, if our call is still going ahead.

Time –55 minutes: E-mail from someone who is confused by daylight saving time, asking where everyone is.

T –15 minutes: E-mail from Marketing Person 1 to remind us that the call is in 15 minutes. Response e-mail from Alpha Male 2 warning that his previous call with Important Customer might not finish on time to join our call. Try to get the ball rolling without me, he says, difficult though it might be.

T +2 minutes: After frantic and unsuccessful attempts to dial in, you call from your mobile using the Slovakian access number. It's just you and a marketing intern on the call. The intern has been instructed by Marketing Person 1 not to say anything during the call. Small talk is difficult.

T +5 minutes: Someone who speaks no English dials in using the Norwegian access number. This may, or may not, be a mistake. Small talk not improving.

T +5 to T +15 minutes: A new person joins each time you get three words into a sentence. Fragments of speech about difficulty of using access codes, and weather in New York/Singapore/Slovakia, occur. Alpha Males 1 and 2 have not joined yet, but seven middle managers you've never heard of are present on the call. They seem to know each other, despite being based on different continents, and exchange opinions about previous relevant conference calls to which you were not invited.

(I hear the opinion that these call-hangers don't contribute. If we look at the conference call as an attempt to make a decision, this is certainly true. On the other hand, their real job is to send e-mails afterwards to a Senior Person which:

1 questions the wisdom of any decision, hinting that it might undermine Senior Person's authority;

2 suggests that Alpha Males 1 and 2 might be unhappy with the outcome agreed on call;

3 subtly implicates you as the cause of both.

This makes sure that any decisions will swiftly be reversed, giving them the opportunity to build a career based on lurking destructively in the background.)

T +15 minutes: Alpha Male 1 joins from airport lounge, and asks us to recap summary of Penguin Pants Project Crisis. Marketing Person 1 attempts to do this, but airport announcements picked up by Alpha Male 1's phone keep cutting in.

T +20 minutes: Alpha Male 2 joins, and tells us to carry on as if he wasn't there.

T +21 minutes: After 10 seconds, Alpha Male 2 announces he hasn't received the agenda for the call from Marketing Person 2. Intern is silently surprised when he is blamed by Marketing Person 2 for this. He is sent to e-mail the document (which he doesn't possess) so that Alpha Male 2 will have the opportunity to learn why he was on the call after we hang up. Alpha Male 2 asks that, in the absence of an agenda, Alpha Male 1 clarifies Marketing Person 1's recap of the summary.

T +25 minutes: Silence.

T +26 minutes: Alpha Male 1 remembers he muted his phone because of airport noise, and starts clarification again, which is twice as long as the recap, which was twice as long as the summary.

T +33 minutes: Alpha Male 2 remembers you are on the call, and asks you for the Penguin Pant Crisis action item options. You list the action item options as quickly as possible. You recommend that we decide, while we are on this call, which action item option to take.

T +35 minutes: Long silence.

T +38 minutes: Alpha Male 1 breaks silence by announcing they are calling his flight, so let's pick this up next week. Call-hangers burst into life to say sycophantic goodbyes to Alpha Male 1, including jokes about performance of local sports teams. Marketing Persons 1 and 2 compete to thank Alpha Male 1 for sparing his time because they know how busy he is, but discover he has already hung up.

T +43 minutes: Marketing Person 1 proudly announces that she has been given access to Alpha Male 1's diary to schedule follow-up call, and suggests a time. Alpha Male 2 says he knows that Alpha Male 1 is not available at that time, because Alpha Male 1 has offered to meet Alpha Male 2's Important Customer. Marketing Person 1 says she has Alpha Male 1's diary in front of her, and Important Customer is not in diary.

T +46 minutes: Alpha Male 2 says he knows that Alpha Male 1 is not available at that time, because Alpha Male 1 has offered to meet Alpha Male 2's Important Customer. Marketing Person 1 says she has Alpha Male 1's diary in front of her, and Important Customer is not in diary.

T +49 minutes: Alpha Male 2 says he knows that Alpha Male 1 is not available at that time, because Alpha Male 1 has offered to meet Alpha Male 2's Important Customer. Marketing Person 1 says she has Alpha Male 1's diary in front of her, and Important Customer is not in diary.

T+52 minutes: Alpha Male 2 politely points out that his agenda hasn't come through yet.

T +54 minutes: Everyone agrees to pencil the meeting depending on Alpha Male 1's availability. Alpha Male 2 points out that Alpha Male 1 is meeting his Important Customer during that hour, so we might be wasting our time.

T +57 minutes: Exaggeratedly polite goodbyes. Marketing Person 2 says we made some great progress today.

T +60 minutes: You are accidentally CCed on an e-mail from call-hanger suggesting that you placed Alpha Male 1 in an awkward position, and that they should revisit any decisions offline before the follow-up call.

When someone on the Pistonheads message board (**http://www.pistonheads.com** if you must) mentioned my views, a commenter called Andy fired back that:

> That blog was the experience of someone who either rarely uses conference calls, or is in an organisation that is c**p at them. We use calls on a daily basis (so much so that most people have their own conference bridge lines) and if managed well they are so much more efficient than email storms and forcing multiple people to drive to another office just so a meeting can be held...

I recognised the sound of a fellow obsessive, and so I followed the link to his blog, which was a list of things that annoyed him. Among them:

> Drivers with 'Child on Board' stickers showing who don't have kids in the car. If the kids aren't in, take the sticker down, he advises.
>
> People who leave front fog lights on when it's not foggy.
>
> The weather.
>
> TV programmes.

I'm not saying he's wrong, but I can't conceive of someone who can be irritated by the inappropriate use of fog lights but manages to remain calm on a conference call. I'm not sure whether to seek his advice or send him to a doctor.

Post-PowerPoint stress disorder

I'm even more mystified that Andy can be upset by TV in general and not mention PowerPoint. He sounds like a man who uses it when he's not shouting random abuse at fellow road users who don't pay attention to their bumper sticker accuracy.

The second part of office life that I'd prefer had never happened: the presentation. It's not exactly pushing the boundaries to say you don't like PowerPoint. Our common dislike has even become a sort of business non-apology apology. When someone says, 'I know the last thing you want is death by PowerPoint ha ha', what they are really saying is, 'Sod you. You're getting 20 slides whether it's the last thing you want or not.'

I was trying to work out how much of my life I have spent looking at PowerPoint slides. Over the past 15 years, as an absolute minimum, I have spent at least three hours a week looking at presentations. If I spend 12 hours a day awake and get Sundays off to sit in the corner crying softly, that's two weeks of every year.

When I got involved with the exciting worlds of business and technology, sitting in a room trying to work out why I am staring at pictures of two racially diverse men shaking hands wasn't how I saw my future.

I earn some of my money presenting webinars, where often the preparation time includes the following conversation:

> ME: What does the slide with the man punching the air in front of the graph with the line going up next to the cloud inside the interlocking oval shapes balancing on the three pillars mean?
>
> VENDOR: *(consults notes)* It's our value proposition.

I've collected four examples of the type of slides that make me as angry as Andy the Pistonhead in the TV department of Comet on a humid afternoon. I know the last thing you want is death by PowerPoint, but I could make that into three bullet points, maybe add a flow chart of my slow descent into fatal madness, perhaps some clip art of a doctor strapping me into the straightjacket...

1 What the hell are you looking at?

Or: why have so many slides got pictures of casually dressed self-consciously ordinary people looking into the middle distance on them? Like the one in Figure 2.3 from Cap Gemini.

Someone recently explained to me, as if to a small child, that slides with people on them seem more human and so help sales. To this, I'd say that having a conversation with the salesperson might be even more human than staring at a random metrosexual man on a screen while that salesperson barks out bullet points in the dark.[5]

I'd also note that the slide is about inventory audits – which the Organisation for Economic Co-operation and Development (OECD)

Figure 2.3 Illustrating the use of a casually dressed self-consciously ordinary man looking into the middle distance

has declared one of the 10 least human things in the developed world.[6]

2 Too much information

If you need three paragraphs to explain the diagram then you didn't draw the bl**dy picture properly. Note to IBM: when you show your diagram to people and they tell you it needs some explanation, don't make the explanation even more opaque than the picture (Figure 2.4).

When I saw this, I just sat there thinking: in IBM's world, there are 'coarse grained' IT services? With what delicious abandon do they name these categories of... thing? I tuned out for the explanation of the blobs.

3 What are you graphing against what?

I'm a bit of a graphs nerd, but I like to keep them simple. But I'm talking about diagrams with the structure of something along the bottom and then two different categories up the sides and then

Figure 2.4 The explanation is even more opaque than the picture

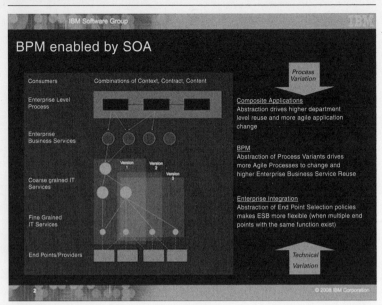

Source: IBM

Figure 2.5 A far from simple graph

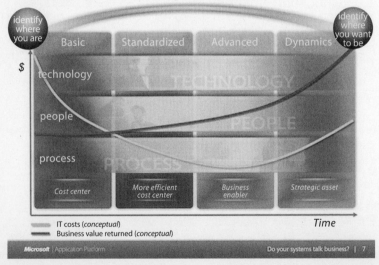

layers of other things at the top and then lines across the middle and then some extra blobs that don't relate to the graph in the top corners (Figure 2.5). This is best done using bright colours or 3-D shapes so that no one notices it makes no sense. The colours imply that, loosely speaking, things are getting better. All PowerPoint slides imply that things have got better (reporting), are getting better (strategising) or will surely get better (fantasising). If things were getting worse, or if it was impossible to fake some good news, no one would do a presentation. They'd slip it out in a low-priority e-mail over Easter weekend.

4 More is more

I know the last thing you want is death by PowerPoint but this next one might just kill you. One day, someone will create the single worst PowerPoint slide ever. Everyone who sees it will be forced to admit that they have wasted their careers staring blankly at lists of lists and pictures they don't understand on a wall, and a revolution of sorts will occur. When it does, Talk Normal will naturally claim the credit. The nearest I could find was the one shown in Figure 2.6: combining elements of all the above, it makes no sense at all in at least five different ways.

Figure 2.6 Is this the worst-ever PowerPoint slide?

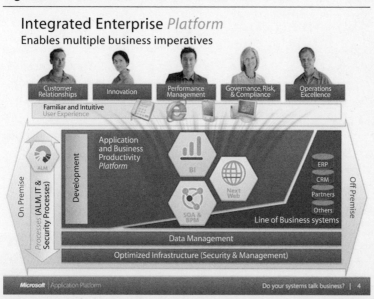

Who are those people and why are they staring at me? Why do the arrows go in the directions they do? How was the central oblong broken up into a two-stage grey slope? Why are there fronds sprouting upwards, or are the happy people being sucked downwards? How did one of the four hexagons escape, and how can we aid its last desperate bid for freedom?

I take comfort only in the knowledge that, though I have lost months of my life looking at these crimes against communication, I'm better off than the poor sap who spent years training as a graphic designer and then ended up having to design them from the frenzied sketches of over-tired executives. Maybe that designer will be inspired to start a movement called Draw Normal, and join up with us.

How HR ruined your life

There are many things that Human Resources does well: it sends out folders full of contracts, makes personal development plans with boxes to tick when we have done things like read the contracts, and tells us why we can't take holiday.

It's not done a great job with finding a name for itself though: Human Resources used to be called 'Personnel', which was a pleasant name, sounded a bit like 'personal', and reminded us that we were those people. HR reminds us that we're a resource.

You could say this is honest, and so Talknormal: that the modern conception of the McJob, in which semi-skilled tasks are automated and deskilled so that wages can be forced down, training becomes optional and short-term staff can be easily replaced, needs an organisation that deals in economic assets rather than personalities. In this way, HR satisfies the principles of Talknormalism.

I'd find the argument more compelling if HR wasn't so stuffed full of fake-happy gibberish. If our workplace is a cult, HR writes the holy books.

Passionate on demand

It starts with recruitment. I received a sad e-mail from a frustrated boss, who was trying to recruit people for a technology public relations firm: 'I have just read a job application where someone writes that they are passionate about corporate communication... in the last few days, three young people in interviews have told me they are passionate about PR or technology. OFGS!', he said. I decided to investigate this excess of passion, which I rarely experience when dealing with their peers in the PR business.

First step: a Google search for the phrase 'Are you passionate about...?', which turned up literally hundreds of job advertisements which begin with this phrase.

Passion seems to be the single most valuable commodity of our times. While we need laws to force recruiters to do things that would help them, but which they seem curiously reluctant to do (300,000 Brits over 50 have been refused a job in the past five years because of their age, even though they might be more experienced and better educated than younger candidates, for example), HR departments are apparently thrilled by anyone who is prepared to declare themselves 'passionate' about a potential job. My correspondent's applicants were just doing what they'd been programmed to do: chuck in a meaningless word to try to win approval.

Where's the harm? If you are selecting applicants based on genuine passion you're also probably going to disqualify the best applicants, because they are the ones who, when you ask if they are 'passionate about vegetables' (a sales development manager job in Hull, £30,000 plus laptop) for example, will say 'Of course not. I'm not mental'.

We all know that the requirement to pretend to be passionate is part of the interview. If you're asked, there's only one answer. We're so anxious to please, we'd express excitement over the prospect of the annual company torturing day.

If you're recruiting at the moment maybe you could spice up your recruitment process by adding a short test with questions like 'Do you find repetitive dull tasks thrilling?', or 'Is being treated like a child extraordinarily motivating for you?' I bet you'd find a large proportion of people who would tick 'yes', simply because it's an interview.

Today's scan of the job boards showed that I could enhance my employability (let's be honest, there's quite a bit of headroom there) if I could bring myself to admit that, yes, I am passionate about 'change control' (I don't know what it is, but apparently a business analyst ought to view it with passion), beer, tax, cake, and telesales. 'IF YES THEN APPLY NOW!!!' the telesales advert screamed at me, hinting that it might be one of those telesales jobs where the ability to bully vulnerable people[7] was the particular type of passion they were looking for.

But thanks to political correctness going mad you can't put that in an advertisement any more. You have to pretend that telesales is about giving people things they actually want, passionately.

I was surprised to find several advertisements asking if I was passionate about recruitment. You'd have thought that recruiters, of all people, would have realised the limitations of asking for fake passion from prospective colleagues. Maybe they just want to attract extremely insincere people. In a recruitment job you might have to lie simultaneously about the employer to the candidate, and the candidate to the employer. This is difficult for most people, but it's probably more accurate to say that it requires a 'passion for commission' than a 'passion for recruitment'.

The go-to resource for mediocre advice, About.com, even has a page of user-supplied answers[8] for the interview question 'What are you passionate about?' I'd suggest that, if you need someone at About.com to tell you the answer to this question, your passion might be lacking an essential element; but then again, if recruiters are so bored that they have to ask you this question, it's probably a cr**py job anyway.

If I ever go to a telesales job interview I'm using this model answer from the article, as suggested by 'Scar':

I'm passionate about everything in the way most people are only passionate about their 'pet' subjects. This is both an advantage and a downfall at times: it means I give 110% to everything I do, whether it's watching paint dry, stuffing envelopes, writing an article or running a company.

Please, please can someone let this guy run a company passionately for us, and tell us how it goes? He's probably available: I looked up 'Are you passionate about watching paint dry?' on the internet and, sad to report, it's one of the few manifestations of passion on demand that recruiters aren't seeking.

All onboard

Another complaint that Talk Normal investigated at around the same time revealed the disturbing growth in the practice of 'onboarding'. 'We are in the process of being "onboarded" as a supplier by a well-

Figure 2.7   The invention of 'onboarding'

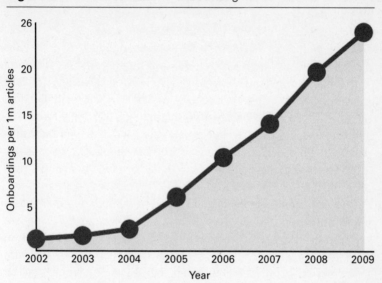

known brand. The people concerned have used this term constantly as a verb, adjective and noun in the last 48 hours. For them it is obviously normal', my complainant revealed.

Onboarding is one of those words that specialist departments think up to dramatise what they do, and make it seem exotic, or military, or difficult. My correspondent was correct to worry: when I checked the mentions of the word in the world's press I discovered that there are more onboarders living and working among us than ever; the most sickening aspect of this grotesque crime against language is that, for them, it's completely normal. Look at Figure 2.7.

That's spectacular growth for a word that has no obvious reason to exist, and which I can't find mentioned at all until 1998. Before 2002, there is one mention of the word for every 10 million published articles in the Factiva database.

The growth is mostly from the sector that the Factiva database of articles calls 'talent management', which is one of those phrases, like 'fresh frozen', where the first word is put there to make impressionable people feel super happy with themselves. Being called 'talent' helps us to be 'passionate'. This also helps people to claim to be self-starting, ambitious, a team player, and all the other phrases that HR puts into job advertisements because they can't think of anything else to say.

The 'talent management sector' produces press releases about onboarding with headlines like: 'Fortune 100 Companies Will Unite at Peopleclick Authoria Global Client Conference to Discuss Business and HR Trends'. Note the use of 'unite', which tries to make a sales conference sound like a protest rally ('What do we want? Onboarding! When do we want it? On receipt of satisfactory references!').

I even found some mentions of offboarding in the last couple of years. As a weasel word for 'sacking' or 'making redundant' it has limitations: imagine calling the victim into your office to explain tactfully that you're offboarding him, and then having to explain what you just said.

Which is my point: HR is meant to deal with us on a human scale, demystifying the corporate cult that we are attempting to join. Instead, it creates its own mystifying jargon, and from the first words of its recruitment advertisement tells us to engage in insincere over-commitment as a condition of acceptance. It's that bad.

For Talknormalists, this is a dilemma – a Jordan Boob Dilemma, if you recall an earlier section of this book. Do you allow yourself to be onboarded in silence, in the knowledge that those who thoughtlessly onboard you today may onboard literally thousands in the future? Or do you speak up?

Role players

Recruitment isn't the only role of HR, of course. Once you are onboarded, it needs to make you feel happy about the horrible mistake you might have made.

This is a difficult task, because our jobs are getting worse. While it has never been more important to be passionate, there's not so much to be passionate about. In 2010, Professor Irena Grugalis of Bradford University School of Management, Odul Bozkurt of Lancaster University Management School and Jeremy Clegg of Leeds University Business School studied UK supermarkets for a report[9] on 'The realities of leadership': 'Almost every aspect of work for every kind of employee, from shopfloor worker... to the general store manager, was set out, standardised and occasionally scripted by the experts at head office.'

Managers manage our emotions instead:

So, what is left for managers to manage? Primarily the answer is 'people management': motivating, beginning with 'getting the day started' meetings they concentrate on meeting targets by, as one manager put it, 'ensuring they (staff) are motivated, trained, they're quick to do the job, and hyped up, and they're going to go out there and deliver'.

Whatever the realities of modern management, language plays a large part in achieving this sad goal. It's not about the work – *The Guardian* pointed out that, according to the National Employer Skills Survey, fewer of us have much influence over how to do our daily tasks than before – down from 57 per cent in 1992 to 43 per cent by 2006 – even though we're regularly told by our employers, our business magazines and our television software adverts that work is a place of exploration and fulfilment.

In short, there's less to be passionate about, but we don't find that out until we've been onboarded. And what are we onboarded to do? Increasingly, we have a 'role'.

When did a job become a role? My guess is, about the time that we started to think of ourselves as the romantic leads in a heroic work-based melodrama, which is about when we started to treat CEOs as philosophers and action heroes rather than businesspeople. Graduating from a job to a role implies we are acting the part rather than just doing something. We're important enough to have an image.

With that image goes an occasional silly job title. This allows companies to advertise their commitment to creativity and fun, at no cost. By making Ronald McDonald chief happiness officer, McDonald's didn't even have to pay a recruiter. And because he's not real (sorry kids), they don't have to do anything except brag about it.

As in any soap opera, in business not all roles are equal. Some hams overact to get attention. For example, a dedicated Talk-normalist passed me details of Steve Lundin at BIGFrontier ('Our event archives provide a walk through the wild west days of Chicago's burgeoning technology scene'), who is apparently the company's Chief Hunter and Gatherer. He's certainly playing a role. You might have an opinion as to what that role is; I'll let you come up with your own description.

Roles are for happy times: research on Factiva shows that, in UK work-related press articles, the roles-to-jobs ratio changed dramatically

Figure 2.8   Phillips Weasel Index: ratio of 'roles' to 'jobs' in UK press, 2001–09

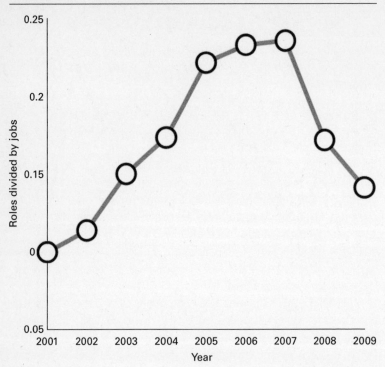

between 2001 and 2007. In 2001 there were about 10 jobs for every role. In 2007, the number of roles peaked: there were only four jobs per role in the press. Then, when the recession hit, the ratio declined to seven jobs per role. The higher this graph went, the more we were writing about roles (Figure 2.8).

Compare the shape of the graph with the Office of National Statistics estimates of UK employment and UK vacancies during the same period (Figure 2.9).

Best to be cautious when drawing a conclusion from this, because more or less every economic graph goes up between 2001 and 2007 and then goes off a cliff. But I'd guess that, when everything seemed exciting and full of promise, we fantasised (and were told) we had an important 'role'. When we were offboarded, it was from our meaningless 'jobs'.

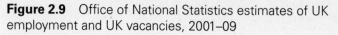

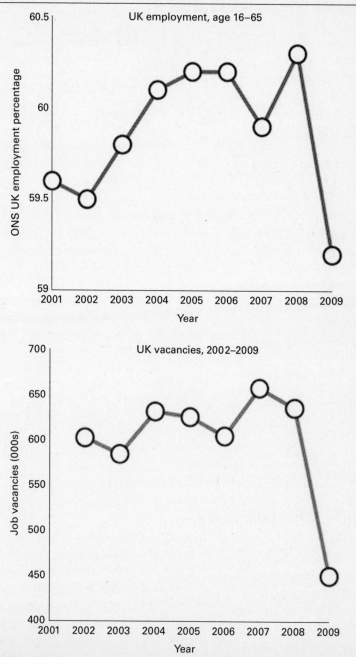# Office Life 67

Figure 2.9 Office of National Statistics estimates of UK employment and UK vacancies, 2001–09

What they say to you, and what they really mean

The idea of a language that removed all words with negative connotations, that created a barrage of declarative sentences so that we didn't need to try to understand too hard, and that was designed to encourage all of us to say 'yes' isn't new. It was pioneered by one of the greatest users of language in the 20th century, and has inspired many people since.

This was the principle behind 'Newspeak', the language used by the totalitarian state in George Orwell's novel *Nineteen Eighty-Four*. Orwell had flirted with the idea of a simplified language (they were all the rage in the 1930s and 1940s), but realised that, once you start messing with the words used to describe the things you see, you begin to see them differently. Therefore the act of changing the language is political – whoever changes it has the power to control the way we think.

It's a bit of a stretch to say that you're all working for Big Brother. That's silly. But there are ways in which the language is subtly re-branded at work to make us feel different about what we do, how we do it and who we work for. It's extremely successful, not least because in these days of the rock-star CEO being interviewed on 24-hour business news, business biographies about how someone saved some company from bankruptcy, 'Town Hall company meetings' and 'personal messages from the board', we have plenty of examples of how we're supposed to sound. We'd not be human if that didn't affect us.

On the other hand, the lack of Talknormalism that results can lead us in some dangerous directions.

Core value judgements

I know the exact moment I decided to give up playing rugby. I was being carried off the pitch on a stretcher with blood pouring out of my head, and one of the prop forwards patted me on the leg and said, 'Well, Tim, looks like your journalism days are over'.

Whether or not you find this joke funny probably depends on whether you think rugby is a noble pursuit for tough people or 80 minutes of institutionalised assault. To tip public perception towards nobility and away from criminality, in 2010 the English Rugby Football Union (RFU) did what the establishment usually does in these cases: made a big statue.

At least when the Victorians did this, they usually had the subtlety to try to hide their hidden agenda. The RFU, with all the subtlety of a prop forward, decided to call the latest addition to the Twickenham furniture the Core Values sculpture.

Why now? I looked it up: 'Two years ago the RFU put together a task group to run an extensive consultation exercise. The Core Values project – the first time a sport has set out to define its value system in formal terms – identified the following principles...'

Speaking as a big fan of Rugby Union, I'm happy to admit it has always had hypocrisy as one of its unspoken core values. The game was proudly amateur when my dad played, and you were banned if you were even suspected of taking money to play – so his club secretly stuffed money in his boot instead.

There have been a lot of people bragging about their core values recently: companies in the United States and the UK are about three times as likely to claim in their press releases that they have core values as they were in 2000, as the three graphs below show.

Can we really have created so many values? I visit a lot of companies, and they appear to have about the same number of values as they had before. They might communicate them a bit more, but three times as much? Some of you must be working in some very ethical companies.

Or, more likely, in some companies which claim to be very ethical.

I thought it might be good to look for the phrase in press releases on military procurement. Defence contractors discovered many more core values during the period between 2003 and 2006 – which is an improvement on the 1990s, when they didn't mention core values at all (Figure 2.10). I shaded the area during which BAE Systems was investigated over accusations of corruption (in 2010 it admitted false accounting and, in a settlement, agreed to pay £257m criminal fines to the United States and £30m to the UK – but the company denies bribery).

Banks, however, had a core value growth peak much earlier (Figure 2.11). This time I shaded a period which covers the Senate Committee of Finance's investigation into Enron, and the complicity of banks in the creative accountancy that took place in that, and other corporate failures.

Figure 2.10 Frequency with which the defence procurement industry mentions 'Core Values'

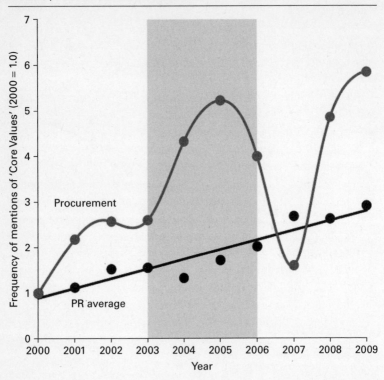

But the real stars of the Core Values Show are in the finance sector: it's the securities business. They didn't make much noise about core values in the past: again, not a single mention of the phrase in the early 1990s that I could find. But they are making up for it now. You are now about six times as likely to read a securities industry press release that mentions core values as you were in 2000. I'm not going to insult you by pointing out which relevant period I've highlighted in the final graph (Figure 2.12).

Of course, my simple measurement doesn't explore what those core values might be. In 2010 I interviewed Dr Doug Hirschhorn, who is one of the top trader coaches in the world. I asked him what the values of his trainees are: 'These people get paid an obscene amount of money. They are not curing cancer or creating new ways to feed people. It draws the sort of people attracted to sensation-seeking', he said.

Figure 2.11 Frequency with which the banking industry mentions 'Core Values'

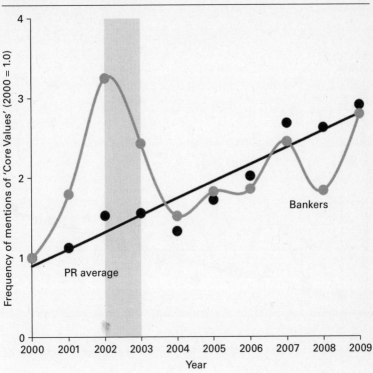

The sensation-seeking search for obscene personal wealth is a core value, I guess. But I'm also guessing that it's not the core value mentioned in those press releases.

Faint traces of buttock

In September 2009 The Times Bugle podcast described an apology by the former CEOs of bailed-out banks in front of a UK parliamentary committee as 'not so much half-a**ed, as containing barely detectable traces of buttock'. At the same time, the CEOs of the large US banks appeared in front of their senior politicians to admit to as little as possible – while approving billions in bonuses from trading in a market created and supported almost entirely by central banks.

Two years on, it's still fair to say that the image of many of the largest organisations in the financial market isn't at an all-time high.

Figure 2.12   Frequency with which the securities industry mentions 'Core Values'

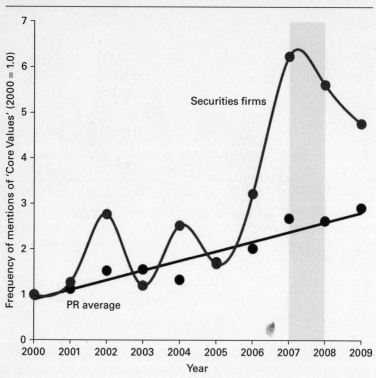

But as the banks appeared to tell us that they were good people really, I decided to investigate what they were writing about corporate social responsibility (CSR).

There are lots of ways to treat CSR. You could view it as corporate whitewash: a company can have active CSR policies while cutting back on safety that makes a natural disaster more likely. You could view it as a fundamental role of 21st-century capitalism: the wealth you create should be balanced against the damage that wealth creation does. You could think of it as a profit centre: back in 2004, The Work Foundation created an influential report that claimed rewards of between 19 and 40 per cent enhanced profitability.

On the one hand, CSR is easy to cut back if money is more important than ethics. On the other, a solid CSR story is a powerful generator of good publicity, which many large companies, with their reputations as tax-dodging, self-centred fat cats, could use.

Figure 2.13   Mentions of CSR in the business press

A quick analysis of the press coverage of CSR through the boom and the bust might tell us something about the motivations to create CSR campaigns. At least, it will tell us what those companies are excited to talk about.

On first look, there was good news in the press coverage of CSR. The consistent rise in the number of stories about it since 2002 continued through the financial crisis. There were about four times as many articles about CSR in 2009 as there were in 2002, which suggests that interest hasn't gone away (Figure 2.13).

But that just counts the number of stories about it. Without reading hundreds of articles, many of them roughly identical, we can't claim that CSR is more popular.

What are these stories about? Business ethics in general have been in the news quite a bit in 2009, yet the number of stories that mentioned CSR alongside ethics or ethical behaviour, and didn't talk about profit, dropped off suddenly when the recession hit (Figure 2.14).

Still, it didn't look too bad; the long-term trend was slightly upward. And this is a rough measure: it would not capture a story in which a global bank CEO argued that ethics are more important than profit, for example. Though I'm pretty sure there wasn't one.

Figure 2.14   CSR: ethics and not profit

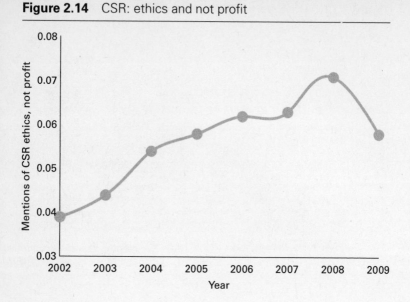

Figure 2.15   CSR: profit and not ethics

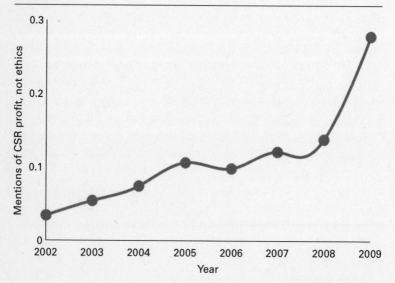

This is interesting: if we look at the similar graph for CSR stories that mention profitability but not ethical behaviour, we see the opposite effect in 2009: a sudden jump (Figure 2.15).

Figure 2.16 CSR: 'ethics' and 'profit' articles compared

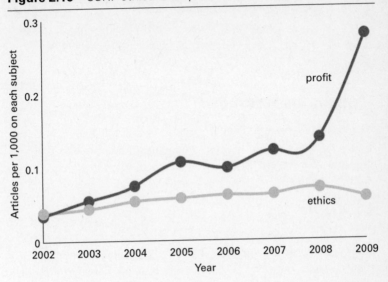

So to see what's really going on, let's overlay the two trends, because in 2002 the frequency was roughly equal (Figure 2.16).

Gosh! Our search is not perfect, but in 2002 there were almost the same number of ethics-not-profit stories as profit-not-ethics stories. Since then the number of ethics-based CSR stories hasn't really shifted, and is now declining. But look at the coverage for CSR-as-profit! That's really taking off.

Before we condemn companies as cynical, a couple of possible explanations: maybe the only way to protect a CSR programme when money is tight is to convince shareholders and CEOs that it is all about making pots of money. Or maybe journalists are just writing stories about balance sheets now, and find business ethics a bit irrelevant, or unfashionable.

In the banking industry in the 12 months between financial crisis and the appearances before the respective sets of politicians (a sector that has been accused both of being ethically challenged and far too motivated by profit), there were 82 stories on CSR that mentioned ethical behaviour, but not profit. There were 548 (six times as many) CSR stories that mentioned profit, but not ethical behaviour.

You might think that business, and especially the financial sector, has often been half-a**ed about its social responsibility, and motivated mainly by the profitability of the idea, not the ethical underpinning. It's not a crime if they are – but it's better if we know. If so, these graphs seem to suggest (in Bugle terms) that the press coverage of those responsibilities has them showing increasingly faint traces of buttock.

Thought followership

I am forever being told that companies are thought leaders in something or other, and that thought leadership encourages recruitment and retention. It probably even makes the canteen food taste better. Thought leadership is indeed a wonderful thing – I'm just not sure who has it.

As one of the blogosphere's true thought leaders, in my mind, on a good day, I imagine the world of thought leadership is something like the graph shown in Figure 2.17. The people who think the most talk the most about thinking, and the circus chisellers who haven't had an original idea in years mostly shut up about it.

I wanted to fit some companies onto my graph, so we can be confident that when they brag to you about their thought leadership

Figure 2.17   The world of thought leadership

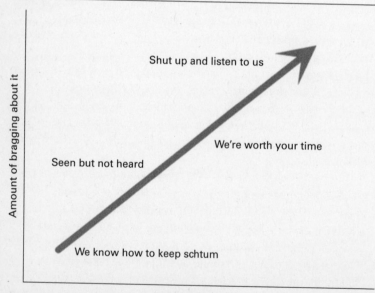

ability, it's not a waste of everyone's time. My first stop: the top 10 of the BusinessWeek Most Innovative Companies List.

Searching for mentions of thought leadership on their corporate websites I was sadly disappointed. Toyota, Nintendo and Nokia had no mention of thought leadership at all. Google, a company that often seems so enthusiastic about its cleverness that it could eat itself, had but a single mention, as did HP. Research in Motion managed four thought leaderships. Apple clocked up 32 mentions – but then I found out that they were all the titles of iTunes Podcasts, and so they don't really count. Microsoft upped the average with 96 mentions.

Only IBM goes big on claiming thought leadership, with 887 mentions of the phrase – but that's because it's a job title in IBM. But cut IBM some slack! That's only one mention for every five patents the company was awarded in 2008 (the most patents in the United States for the gazillionth year in a row), or 177 for every Nobel Prize an IBM employee has won. That's quite a lot of thought with which to lead, I think we can agree.

I note also that, while innovation leader number 10 Wal-Mart couldn't find any actual mentions of thought leadership on its website, it helpfully suggested partial matches – the top one of which was an excellent 'Transformers Revenge of the Fallen Autobot' ($35 plus postage, in stock). We can only marvel at Wal-Mart's desperation to make a sale, no matter how irrelevant, to absolutely anyone who visits its site.

So, to reliably find people who will claim thought leadership, I needed to look further down the innovationary league table. I went to the natural home of the barely innovative: that's right, I searched for companies who claimed to be thought leaders in their press releases. Bingo! You can keep your Nobel prizes IBM, here's the motherlode. A few highlights from the two days previous to my search:

- You'll be delighted to hear that thought leader Bentley 'Introduces Timely Value-Creative Subscription Innovations to Help Sustain the Infrastructure Professions'.

- When we think about thought leaders in pharmacy benefit management, of course we think of Prime Therapeutics LLC, which 'Receives 2010 TIPPS Certification for Adherence to High Transparency Standards'.

- If you strive to discover thought leadership in the hotly contested wound-care field, the newly announced 'Systagenix Medical Advisory Board' is apparently where you should seek it.

- The comprehensively named Everything Channel has announced that it will launch 'A new sub-group group within Channelweb Connect'. 'We hope that this new group will help drive conversation with thought leaders in the solution provider community', it says. A must for those who value thought leadership within sub-group groups.

On this evidence, you might find the graph of genuine innovation vs amount of noise made is a more accurate reflection of the world in which we live (Figure 2.18).

Note that I've marked an area which combines minimum thought and maximum bragging as the 'STFU Zone'. If you're in this zone and are thinking about f**ting out another press release about thought leadership, take the hint.

Figure 2.18 Genuine innovation vs amount of noise made – a more accurate reflection of the world?

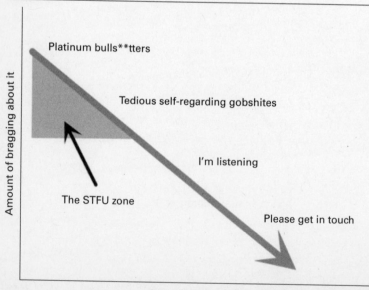

Talknormalise me

What can we do to stand against this tide of tedium? The problem that most of us face is that we don't call the meeting, or arrange the call, or write the presentation. But, when we do have the chance, how can we make it interesting?

The Doughnut of Excitement

Imagine a ring doughnut. It is not an ordinary doughnut. It is the Talk Normal Doughnut of Excitement. Draw it on a piece of paper (Figure 2.19).

Now imagine that I can put a cross on this paper, depending on how interesting what you just said was. The closer I get to the middle of the doughnut, the less exciting it is to me. Say at the point X, shown in Figure 2.20.

What you just said is as dull as it could possibly be. When you tell me that world peace would be a good thing, when I hear that customer service is important, when your manager tells you that, as an employee, you are part of your company's biggest asset, we're in the middle of the hole in the middle of the doughnut.

If you find yourself in that hole, don't worry. As long as we get out of it, we're fine. We need to get out of the hole, because anyone can say these things, no one needs to act differently or even think about

Figure 2.19   The Talk Normal Doughnut of Excitement

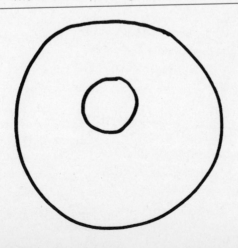

Figure 2.20   The closer the X to the middle of the doughnut, the less exciting it is

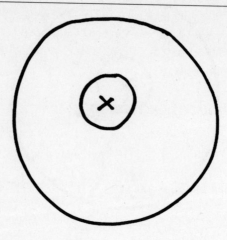

them after they have been said, and they waste a lot of time. It's like discussing the weather.

Problem is, the first thing that pops into your head is a middle-of-the-doughnut thought. Listen to someone being interviewed on the news: take away the first 15 seconds of most answers, and they'd be much more interesting.

So, when we have the chance to prepare what we say or write, we have to travel along this line, out of the hole and into the doughnut. The further we go along it, the more interesting we become (Figure 2.21).

What happens, you might say, when we leave the doughnut altogether? That's the stuff that is interesting, but irrelevant. You decide where the edge of your doughnut is (Figure 2.22). Your company has a corporate doughnut, even if it doesn't know it. For example, it doesn't tell everyone what you earn, although they would be pretty interested in it.

So we want to get to point A. What gets us there? Two things. Talk with precision, and talk about real life instead of concepts.

Precision: we dealt with the problem of the word 'significant' earlier. A quiz: how large is a 'significant uplift' in sales? How long is a 'significant time'? How much money is a 'significant discount'? We have no idea, especially if the person doesn't have the opportunity to ask.

Figure 2.21 Travelling out of the hole and into the doughnut

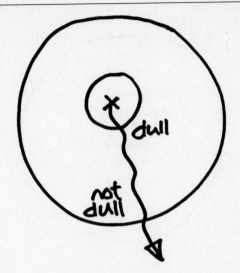

Figure 2.22 Deciding where the edge of the doughnut is

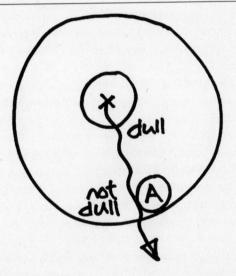

If I tell you that the UK Royal Society for the Prevention of Accidents reports that a significant number of people attend hospital each year thanks to accidents with a bird bath in the UK, how many do you think it is? Chances are, if I tell you that every year it is more than 400, that's probably more exciting.

The temptation to be non-specific is especially strong when we are delivering bad news: but remember, bad news equals fear. Fear gets exaggerated. 'A small number of redundancies' will likely be exaggerated, whereas the precise number cannot.

The second ingredient of doughnut-based excitement is real life. At home we deal with concrete events and actions, their effects and consequences. We use anecdotes and stories. At work we often retreat behind concepts and segments. We don't talk about 'businesses with fewer than 50 people working in them'; we talk about SMBs. Few people think: I'm an SMB.

Also, we talk about how we must strategise and evaluate, but not what we should do. How should we act, and how will we know it's the right thing to do?

An example: I've just been told that companies that want to improve their security should audit their requirements, decide what resources to commit and create a policy. I have no idea what the audit should measure, what resources are, what I could do with them, what should be in the policy, what happens when people don't follow it, and why.

Contrast with this: if someone asked you, 'How do I know if she doesn't fancy me?' you wouldn't tell him to establish a Potential Girlfriend Monitoring Matrix, score the Potential Attraction Indicators, and Create Strategic Relationship Enhancement Milestones. You'd say: 'Does she always bring her best mate along when you go out?' If the answer's yes, your friend won't need those Strategic Milestones.

Worst of all, don't say: 'For a long-term commitment-based relationship, significant attraction is preferable if not essential.' Middle of the doughnut means no friends at home.

Sensing that the concept was Licensed to Enthrall, Ian Fleming even explained the Doughnut of Excitement in the James Bond novel *The Spy Who Loved Me* – staging a brief respite from sex and violence so that a local newspaper editor could explain how to write about bus timetables. Unsurprisingly, they didn't put this bit in any of the films:

'Conductors on the Number 11 service complain they have to work
    too tight a schedule...'
Len put his pencil through it.
'People, people, people! This is how it ought to go: "Frank
    Donaldson, a wide-awake young man of 27, has a wife, Gracie

and two children... 'I haven't seen my kids in the evening since the summer holidays,' he told me, 'ever since these new schedules came in.'" There are people driving these buses. They're more interesting than the buses.'

The Doughnut of Excitement is not just for presentations, formal documents. Too often our office communication is sullied by vagueness. If you are a senior manager, never, even when you are stressed or annoyed, say, 'I need the report immediately or you're offboarded.' Instead say, 'I need the report before 4.15 pm or you will be marched to your desk by security, forced to put your pathetic possessions into a cardboard box, and escorted from the premises.' It takes longer to say, but you'll have no trouble holding the attention of your audience. Precision makes a simple statement of fact more informative, which your colleagues will admire and appreciate.

A special note for the professional classes

Excessive precision with too much abstraction is the worst combination of all.

For lawyers, for example, it's often a requirement of the profession. Much of the professional jargon is based around the abstraction of concepts, and that can mean that what you say isn't hard to understand, it's impossible. Doctors struggle with this every day, with variable results.

Jargon is especially the problem of the professional classes: people whose professions are, by definition, hard to enter, and where entry is impossible without a minimum level of knowledge. The knowledge is expressed in jargon; the exclusivity is expressed when they use the jargon on us, watching our mystified faces.

It's not necessarily aggression: when you talk to other people who are like you all day, you forget that outsiders see the world differently. Not in Latin, for starters.

I don't care what you think: I like many lawyers. They can be witty, interesting people. They hold conferences in nice hotels and sometimes ask me to speak. Usually they're polite afterwards. And get lawyers talking about something that isn't the law, and often they are funny and clever.

Also, for a jobbing freelance, law firms pay well and usually have excellent biscuits when you visit them. I went for a meeting in one firm's office and a chef in a tall hat came to ask me what I wanted for lunch. Another firm has by far the best pencils I have ever used in its meeting rooms (at least it did until they left me alone for five minutes).

But if you're editing copy for them, they don't half make you earn the money. Lawyers write like badly programmed jargonbots. Here's a paragraph that I was asked to fix up a while ago for a business magazine:

> Section 217 of the Companies Act 2006 provides that (except in the case of a bona fide termination payment) it is unlawful for a company to make payment to any of its directors by way of compensation for loss of office, or as consideration for or in connection with their retirement from office, without particulars of the proposed payment (including its amount) being disclosed to, and approved by ordinary resolution of, the members of the company.

No, I don't either.

I've learned that it is basically pointless offering advice to lawyers on how to write like a journalist. Maybe that is because they're earning 10 times as much as me, so it's understandable if they don't really see an urgent need to adapt to my way of thinking. It's more useful for me to pass on a few tips on how the rest of us can write like a lawyer, and urge you to do the opposite of the next six things I recommend.

In my experience, many of the same rules apply to teachers, engineers, police officers, planning officers, surveyors and sometimes doctors:

1 If you don't want to be easily understood, Latin is always better than English. When writing for a general reader I can tell you *a priori* that *inter alia* it's your *erga omnes* right to stick in a few phrases in a language that they don't understand, just so they know who's the daddy. After all, *nulla poena sine lege*. I have no idea what I've just typed.

2 Qualify every statement no matter how meaningless. A rule of thumb: never use fewer than four clauses in each sentence, and don't use full stops when there are perfectly good commas going to waste. If you used short sentences then people would be able to read your article out loud to peasants;

and then poor illiterate people would understand your argument and your status would be forever compromised.

3   Ultimately, sit on the fence. Real advice has to be paid for, so make anything written for non-payers look like you're going to help them right up to the last sentence – then don't. Useful final-paragraph phrases for appearing to be helpful while being no bl**dy use at all, include telling us that we should keep a watching brief rather than actually do anything, or that we might also give careful consideration to something you haven't previously mentioned, or that we could usefully keep abreast of whatever it is that you're supposed to have made us abreast of in the preceding six paragraphs. Not many people will complain, because few of them will have made it this far anyway.

4   Use the passive voice where at all possible. It will be seen that this may possess utility. Paragraphs should be drawn up by the lawyers concerned only after careful consideration of this advice. Articles composed in this fashion will be credited with education and poshness – by other lawyers, anyway. Other people ask why you are writing in this weird way. Ignore them! Or should I say: endeavour to ensure that they are ignored.

5   Favour obsolete words. Keep a stock of aforementioneds, hereinafters, forthwiths and herebys, and use them to give your prose the authentic feel of the 18th century.

6   Most important: never take advice on this subject from people who are not lawyers.

Notes

1   Gossip with each other using instant messaging instead of doing our work.
2   http://bit.ly/shutdownfest
3   Download it here: http://bit.ly/consultconsult
4   When I first wrote about this in 2010, I got a sudden surge of e-mail from readers admitting that 'this is exactly my experience'. I checked who was reading the post that day, and a huge proportion of Talk Normal's hits were from the European Commission. Just saying.

5   This is not true when the appeal is highly emotional (unlike here). The University of Oregon found, for example, that we are more likely to donate to charity if we see a picture of one starving girl than if we are given statistics about a much larger famine elsewhere. We even donate less when there are statistics alongside the picture. So next time you present, experiment: prepare a deck where a small dog is being threatened by a gun and shout 'buy my stuff or the puppy gets it'. Let me know what happens.

6   Made up stat, alas. But it doesn't mean it's not true.

7   'A WHISTLEBLOWER today reveals the shocking rules given to telesales staff raising charity cash for Cancer Research UK. The ex-trainee cold-caller told how she was told to: PESTER people for money three times per call, as contracted. TARGET people battling cancer. BULLY students, OAPs and jobless people to hand over cash they couldn't afford; and was TICKED OFF for failing to push for a donation from a partially disabled, confused 92-year-old.' *The Mirror*, 23 September, 2009.

8   http://bit.ly/fakepassion

9   SKOPE Research Paper No 91 'No place to hide? The realities of leadership in UK supermarkets'.

3 Mediocre media

The old school

Sir Harold Evans, editor of *The Sunday Times* from 1967 to 1981, and editor of *The Times* from 1981 to 1982, wrote the book on how to be a good journalist. *Essential English for Journalists, Editors and Writers* (see Appendix) is an excellent manual, with examples of good and bad writing, practical advice, and clear explanations of why the guidelines are important.

It even has lists of phrases to avoid: 'value judgement' doesn't need the first word, 'pare down' doesn't need the second, 'in the city of Manchester' doesn't need the middle three.

When I started as a journalist the first company I worked for had an old newspaper man called Harold who ruled the newsroom. He was called chief sub-editor – the 'sub' is the person who fixes your mistakes before they go into the newspaper or magazine – although it was inconceivable that anyone could have worked under him.

Every morning he would arrive at 4 am and edit all the copy, looking for these mistakes, and a thousand more that he had internalised in the 50 years to that date. If you made unnecessary errors, he'd call you in to his cubbyhole and shout at you in front of your mates, while you stared at his one remaining front tooth as it wobbled precariously.

Harold had the final say on all matters of style and choices of word. This didn't always work well: he insisted that the headline of a review of a product called Eagle should be changed from 'The Eagle has landed' to 'The Eagle has alighted'. But we had someone who set rules, and enforced them: I would expect a call into the office if I began a sentence with 'but'.

We also learned that, just because we had written our story in a certain way, that wasn't the way in which it should be published. Sometimes half the article would be deleted, the fourth paragraph moved to the front, the last sentence of every paragraph lopped off.

We had good reason to do this: printing was expensive, so there wasn't much room in the magazine for waffle. Internet publishing has removed this restriction, but it isn't always a good thing. We can write stories that are as long as we like instead of keeping them to 250 words.

We have also largely done away with our subs. It's like having a revolution and then wondering what to do next: while the immediate reaction is joy, because there is one less person to make sarcastic remarks while putting a line through your funniest joke, we have to rely on ourselves. The results are not always optimal.

There is no time to Talk Normal

This is complicated by our impatience. Stories that took a day to write – because nothing could be published until the next morning – are now published in minutes. 'We should be getting breaking news up within five minutes', said a memo to BBC News Interactive in 2005. 'I don't normally spend more than an hour on a story. Otherwise I wouldn't be able to write so many', was the complaint of a PA news-wire correspondent at the same time[1] (PA is a news agency – it writes hundreds of stories a day, which are the raw material that newspapers and websites routinely use). Inevitably this means that news has more emotion, less considered thought, and relies more on gossip than before.

It's not that newspapers used to be perfect: 150 years ago it was often difficult to work out what a story was actually about, let alone what had happened. But it is an important change because there is more 'journalism' than ever before: when there's a big news story, we can Google ten versions of it in five minutes. We don't always check the source of these stories, and we don't know how experienced the writer is, or how much expertise the writer has on the subject.

This rush to publish means that there is little time for quality control, which affects all of us. Often, marketing material that companies send to a publishing company – for example press releases designed solely to brag – is published verbatim. Hyperbolic excitement and jargon are just repeated, rather than being translated so that we understand the meaning and context.

Essential English for Journalists repeats the old joke about word economy: a fishmonger who advertised 'Fresh Fish Sold Here' had a friend who insisted he rub out 'Fresh', because it was obviously fresh, and 'Here' because if you have a shop, it's obvious where you sell your fish. Then he rubbed out 'sold', because no one would give away their fish. Then he deleted 'Fish', because everyone could smell it.

You can go too far when you're editing. You can be too strict, and insist that eagles alight. But increasingly we're reading stories that tell us less than they seem.

This section is about four roles of the media: explaining, entertaining, telling us what to think, and – this is a new one – building communities, and how the retreat from Talknormalism has affected their ability to do that.

The explainers

Whether there's a nuclear reactor melting down, thousands demonstrating in the streets of a foreign city that we can't point to on a map, or banks collapsing with gazillions of debt, we rely on media to explain to us.

When the invasion of Iraq began in 2003, I was in the United States, and watched the saturated news coverage. As we now know, the US military had given access to 'embedded' journalists – asked them to join in, as long as they didn't touch anything – and the journalists did a wonderful job in conveying what it was like to be inside a tank, or the noise that exploding things made, or the food that soldiers ate. It didn't mean there was much time for showing boring things like maps, for example, so we had no idea where the tanks were. But BOOM POW BANG POP.

One report even attached a camera to the turret of a tank, so you could see it lining up its shot. It was just like a computer game, though games have better graphics.

It's an example of how, when there's not much time and not much appetite for analysis, the job of media to explain what's going on is put to one side so that we can KABOOM KABOOM WOW LOOK AT THAT! WHERE DID THE BUILDING GO?

Wars are a good example of this trend, but in all news there's a line between simplification and oversimplification – and we regularly cross it.

Shooting the messengers

It's always easy to blame PR companies and their often laughable press releases for the pain of irritating jargon. In the UK, at least, that's not the end of the story.

The first responsibility of a journalist is to extract jargon, which most people can't understand, and explain it in words that we can understand. It's not enough just to pass the problem on to us. Although old Harold was a very irritating man, he didn't let us slip jargon words past him because we didn't understand them.

I did some research which measured the frequency of the seven most pernicious jargon phrases[2] identified in David Meerman Scott's Gobbledygook Manifesto[3] in 2006, which I will later use to discover the Worst Press Release in History. I looked at the frequency of these seven jargon phrases since 1990 in press releases – which are companies simply talking about themselves, and in which they can say anything they like – and the news stories which are written as a result of those press releases.

When the media is working properly to explain the world around us, it doesn't delight in the word porn of jargon-filled press releases. I have read hundreds of thousands of these press releases, though increasingly I have to admit I glaze over after the first couple of lines, and they're a lesson in what happens when you allow companies to talk about themselves.

In the graphs below, each blob maps the relative frequency of a jargon phrase in one year between 1990 and 2009. If it's on the diagonal line, it appears equally frequently in newspapers and press releases in that year. Below the diagonal line, and the phrase is more frequent in press releases. Above it, and it's more frequent in the press. I used only major news sources and newswires, not geeky jargon-filled magazines.

In the last section I criticised the US news media for not covering a war in the way I wanted it to. Some might detect that I'm veering into knee-jerk anti-Americanism here, and that soon I will start complaining that they can't even spell aluminium (although 'aluminum' was the original spelling used by British chemist Humphry Davy in 1812), and that Americans ask us to 'deplane' when we land at their airports (this is a legitimate cause for concern, you must agree).

On the other hand, the US media is doing a terrific job of stamping down on these seven jargon phrases, and has been doing a terrific job consistently for 20 years. Look at the graph shown in Figure 3.1, and imagine the sub-editor has stamped on the jargon with a big boot.

Figure 3.1 Comparison of frequency of seven common jargon phrases between US news sources and press releases, 1990–2009

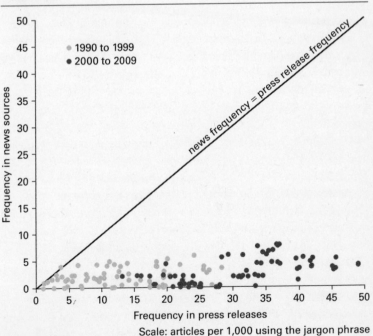

Scale: articles per 1,000 using the jargon phrase

Source: Factiva

That's exactly what newspapers should be doing. It's what we should all be doing, but it's up to the people who are paid to do this to set an example.

And so we come to the British press, with its reputation for clarity and insight, with its journalists who stop at nothing to get the story, with its mission to explain to the common man, and with the inheritors of the standards of old Harold and his generation ensuring that standards are upheld. Are they?

Here's the same graph for the UK press (Figure 3.2).

There's no jargon-weeding going on, at least for these seven phrases. In the Gobbledygook manifesto, it was journalists who picked the seven jargon phrases in the first place, so we know that they recognise them, and are as irritated by them as Talknormalists like us. It's just that they aren't doing anything to solve the problem.

So the conclusion that I draw is that, if a journalist's job is partly about weeding out jargon from its raw material, US journalists are doing a good job and British journalists are doing a rubbish one.

Formula for failure

If N is the number of column inches, R is the relevance to current news obsessions, I is the importance of the academic whose name is attached to the press release and ∂ is a Greek character that I introduced to make the whole thing look like it came from a university rather than the desk of a public relations consultant, then the formula for press coverage of a made-up scientific formula is too depressing to invent.

In 2009 I visited the British Science Festival to interview journalist and author Dr Simon Singh, who had presented a speech to the academics gathered there called 'Why Journalists Love Stupid Equations and Other Problems in the Media'. His problem: made-up formulas, which are a wonderful tool for a journalist who wants a quick and easy story, and an excellent example of how something that looks like it is explaining the world to us is really doing the opposite.

If you have been under a rock and so missed the stupid equation trend, over at an excellent blog called Apathy Sketchpad there's a collection of the most miserable 'formula for' stories.[4] These include the formulae for the perfect sitcom (including the variable 'how often someone falls over'), apparently concocted by neuroscientist

Figure 3.2 Comparison of frequency of seven common jargon phrases between UK news sources and press releases, 1990–2009

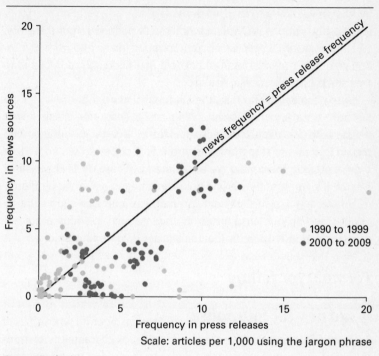

Source: Factiva

Dr Helen Pilcher, and for the perfect day, which somehow manages to avoid factoring in things like the state of the economy, or more or less anything that would affect your mood, also apparently created by a scientist.

Then there's the *Sun* newspaper's story on the formula which tells us if your boob line is too low – which, when you put numbers into doesn't even work.

I declare an interest: a few years ago I was called in by a F pany to work out why the newspapers had stopped printi for their price comparison website client. The answer they did was make up increasingly asinine formulae f freesheets and women's magazines. At the time t ately pushing 'the formula for a perfect bargain' up), which had half a dozen variables to consider, a number between 100 and 700 which you had to compare to a table of results. You were meant to use this calculation while staring into a shop window, and they couldn't even be bothered to (or didn't know how to) make it come out as a percentage.

Even the journalists who had obediently printed their other formulae realised this was so idiotic that they wouldn't touch it. When I pointed this out, the account director explained to me that this is what newspaper readers needed.

I suggested to Singh that naming the PR companies who rely on this guff might act as a deterrent. 'Problem is, if you name them, then people who want to get in the papers are going to say, fantastic, we should go to that PR company', he pointed out.

Like an internet survey of 23 people, or the story of how some type of vegetable will save you from cancer, the fake formula offends me because it is cynical lowest-common-denominator PR. It offends me because as journalists we all know this is c**p – but we publish it anyway. And it offends me because we assume this is all the science that readers can tolerate without their heads exploding while they're reading the paper.

A sad day for journalism

A particular example of this is the continuing popularity of Blue Monday, a fake formula designed to calculate the most depressing day of the year. It certainly is for me, as every year I get to read the same tired blog posts and retread newspaper articles.

The annual attack of the Blue Monday idiots is a depressing time for Talknormalists. In 2011 it was as bad as ever. It started when a PR company e-mailed me, because they knew how much I hated this day, to ask when it was. They were preparing a press release to capitalise on Blue Monday, they explained, and just wanted to check they had read the formula correctly.

I pointed out that the formula could be read in any way you wanted it to, but it was fixed to make Blue Monday the last Monday in January. In effect, it works back from a conclusion. The conclusion (the date) was fixed so that companies could market their products around it. It's sort of a post-Christmas Christmas for lazy public relations executives.

The day became more depressing when a colleague whom I suspected came to tell me that it was Blue Monday. He wanted to make sure I was aware of this breakthrough, because he knew I had a science education, and there was a formula in the newspaper.

Imagine! A formula in a newspaper. It's like seeing a talking dog.

We must look on the bright side. For students of the asinine, Blue Monday has a lot to offer:

1 There are often two Blue Mondays in the press on consecutive weeks. This could be a demonstration of how the scientific method means our knowledge advances in small steps; its conclusions should not be taken as revealed truth; they are merely suppositions based on the best evidence that we have today. We should welcome uncertainty as a stimulus for debate and further research.

2 On the other hand, it might just mean that one PR company timed its campaign a week earlier than the other, and the equation is so vague and subjective that you can fit it to more or less any day of the year if you try hard enough.

3 For once, we know whom to put in the stocks and throw fruit at. Dr Ben Goldacre, who writes the 'Bad Science' blog, did the real research on this when the equation first showed up. Blue Monday was invented by Porter Novelli ('We have the right conversations with the right people at the right time') in 2006 for Sky Travel. The idea of the equation was shopped around academics, offering them money if they claimed to have derived it. Dr Cliff Arnall, at the time a temporary lecturer at the Cardiff University Centre for Lifelong Learning, grabbed the opportunity and made some good publicity for himself – though his former employers seem less delighted by this, and have politely distanced themselves from this style of scientific publication. Dr Arnall has no genuine insight into the day when you are least happy, but at least he has 'Dr' in front of his name. If we could only get a picture of him in a white coat, then Blue Monday would be so much more credible.

4 How do we give depression more pizazz? The question has been asked in a thousand marketing brainstorms. One genuinely sad aspect of Blue Monday every year is the miserable attempt by some PR companies to inject pep into unhappiness by telling us to buy something.

Recall that the whole sham was set up to sell holidays; other people use it as an excuse to bung out a lightweight 'why not buy this?' press release – just as long as they don't get too hung up on the depression thing. For example: 'Blue Monday is believed to highlight a more general temporary gloominess for a usually more balanced and positive population', says Caroline Carr, hypnotherapist and author of the just published Living with Depression.

General temporary gloominess: translation – 'as a therapist, how can I describe this fictional marketing construct as if it was real so that I can plug my book without overstepping any kind of regulatory guidelines?'[5]

Journalists trot out exactly the same Blue Monday feature every year, partly because the end of January is pretty barren if you're looking to fill the inside of a local paper. You did detox diets, giving up smoking and gym membership in week one, and it's not time to do 'Put some spark into your love life with these Valentine's Day ideas' yet. Those lifestyle pages don't fill themselves, you know.

I don't like to miss out on a misery party and so I feel the urge to explain my personal general temporary gloominess using an equation. After as much as 30 seconds of careful research, I came up with this:

$$D = \left[\sum_{i=1}^{\infty} c_i + E^2 \right] \times \delta$$

where D is how depressed I will feel

c_i is the number of column inches given to article a_i where $i = 1, 2, 3, \ldots$

E is the number of times they mention that stupid equation

and δ is the number of days that this story lasts.

If you want to use my formula in a meaningless and generic story about how bloggers get sad once a year when they read press releases about Blue Monday, please quote me as 'Dr Tim Phillips, an expert in disappointment at the Polytechnic of Cynicism'. Worse than nothing.

Made-up equations are the closest that many journalists get to anything with statistics in it. This, too, has consequences for our ability to understand what's going on in the world around us (Figure 3.3).

Figure 3.3 The consequences of made-up equations for understanding the world

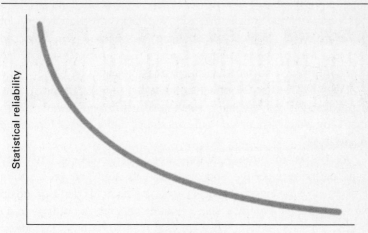

In conversation with David Spiegelhalter, Professor of the Public Understanding of Risk at the University of Cambridge, he admitted to me that he shouts at the TV when they use statistics that scare or confuse us without helping us.

There are plenty of stats that use percentages or relative like-lihoods to compare stuff (before versus after, or this versus that), without really giving us a clue. An example: if you drive 10 miles to buy a lottery ticket, you are between 3 and 20 times more likely to die in a car wreck than win the lottery.

There are even more that sound terrific; they're just not true. An example: a Google search has the same carbon footprint as boiling a kettle.

The answer to this is not, as my mum pointed out, that you can buy lottery tickets online these days, so it's safer than it used to be. Comparing the risk of driving (from which, every time you don't die, you usually get a benefit) and the reward for buying a lottery ticket is like comparing a gun with a gnu because they use the same letters.

The professor would rather we stuck to presenting statistics, where possible, as what would happen to a set of people (10, 100, or for rare events, 1,000). For example, according to the Office for National Statistics, for every 1,000 people who died in 2008, around

Figure 3.4 For every 10 people who come to Talk Normal from a search engine, two arrive following the search for either 'naked' or 'naked people'

330 died from circulatory (heart) disease – and only five in transport accidents. This might imply that overweight gamblers will live longer if they walk or jog to buy a lottery ticket than driving to get it.

I don't understand why magazines and newspapers – and marketing departments and think tanks – don't have a rigid 'house style' (a set of rules that all writers must follow) on how statistics are presented – for example, insisting that spokespeople qualify 'up by 20 per cent' statements with what the expected outcome would be in terms of death, or euros, or gnus (plus a confidence limit).

Newspaper style books have pages about the correct title for a judge and whether you can use aggravate as a synonym for irritate, but I've never seen one with instructions on comparative statistics. Maybe it's because the people who compile style guides know a lot about the meaning of words, but less about the meaning of numbers.

It's not as if the 'for every X people' stat isn't visual enough. For example, I can give you the interesting (and true) statistic that for every 10 people who come to Talk Normal from a search engine, two arrive following the search for either 'naked' or 'naked people', thanks to my using the word on the blog (Figure 3.4).

In many cases, the problem isn't incompetent statistics, it is a lack of trust in observable truth – especially when it gets in the way of a good story. This problem is accentuated by the large number of opinion columnists and blogs, where a one-eyed version of the 'truth' is acceptable.

For example, consider an article written by Joanna Blythman in *The Herald* in Scotland called 'Scientists must not dictate on public health matters' (better leave that job, it seems, to Joanna Blythman). While complaining about Professor David Nutt, who was forced to resign from his job as a drugs adviser after some correct but politically naïve comments about the relative harm of different drugs, she tells us that scientists think their knowledge 'is superior to other types of knowledge we might bring to bear on our decisions, such as intuition, experience, observation, or even common sense'.

Note that intuition is not what a fuddy-duddy old scientist would call 'knowledge'. And as scientists say: the singular of data is not 'anecdote'.

This is aimed at Professor Nutt, who seems to have used all of Blythman's four ways to gather knowledge, plus scientific method too. She's a skilled polemicist: 'The huffing and puffing of Nutt and his indignant allies has obscured the fact that whatever the rest of society thinks or knows about cannabis...', she continues. Note: 'thinks or knows'. As in, if Joanna Blythman thinks something, and has used intuition and some of the other three, then she knows it, so it must be better than anything a scientist has boiled up in a laboratory. Especially if she disagrees with that scientist.

It doesn't stop her throwing around a few stats at the end to make her point that the only scientists who know about statistics are the ones who produce statistics she likes. For example: 'Now we learn, once again from bona fide scientific research, that pregnant women taking folic acid supplements are up to 30% more likely to produce babies with asthma. Yet still the folic acid lobby is arguing that we should press on regardless with blanket fortification of bread and continue to advocate supplements during pregnancy...'

And that, ladies and gentlemen, is how to use statistics to confuse people. Quite apart from the fact that she neglects to point out that the research isn't from a random sample and shows a weak correlation,[6] that a lack of folic acid causes spina bifida and other problems, we don't have a chart that shows this 'up to 30%' as an outcome for 1,000 babies born today.

We can't draw a conclusion, because so far this research doesn't tell us enough with enough certainty. On the other hand, we know a lot about the damage caused to babies by poor nutrition during pregnancy.

One of the problems with the presentation of statistics in the press is that you can always slice the results to be more dramatic than they really are, and that suits a columnist like Blythman.

Actually, it suits our communications culture. There are enough poorly researched statistics out there that we can grab the ones that look best, draw a big pie chart and present it as proof, secure in the knowledge that most of your audience isn't going to be able to ask: How were those figures compiled? How many people were asked? How certain are we that this causes that? What about alternative hypotheses – are they less likely?

Marketers, politicians and journalists who don't know much about numbers know how to do this. Some are genuinely naïve, and don't understand that it's much harder to 'prove' something causes something else than it is to establish there's no relationship between them, or that a big number on its own doesn't mean anything.

If you want to be able to shout at the TV like Professor Spiegelhalter, start by reading *Innumeracy: Mathematical Illiteracy and its Consequences*, by John Allen Paulos, Vintage Books (1990). It's an old book, but numbers – unlike jargon – never go out of fashion. Paulos is a respected mathematician, but he has the knack of writing in a way that almost anyone could understand. He rightly cares that, while illiteracy is condemned, innumeracy is tolerated or even celebrated. Also, the classic *How to Lie with Statistics*, written by Darrell Huff in 1954 (Penguin) is easy to read. We can't change how people lie to us (yet), but at least we can know when it's happening.

I can't help thinking that in-house standards for newspapers, for example, on how they present statistics are far more important than pages of rules on how to refer to the wife of a marquess or an earl.[7] This will come, but not until the people who mislead us because it makes their argument more exciting are brought to heel.

The end of days

As this book goes to press the British government is discussing whether to change the May public holiday in favour of St George's Day (23 April) or the mysterious 'Trafalgar Day' in October. It's a cunning ploy to lure tourists to the UK early and late in the year.

'An autumn bank holiday would not only help the industry but give us all a new focus for celebrating the best of what Britain does', said Tourism Minister John Penrose, to the *Sun* newspaper. We kill dragons and fight sea battles: if we restaged either, I'd buy a ticket.

On this basis, it's just more evidence that British tourism is driven by grim optimism, especially if they want to put a public holiday in October, when the average temperature is 11 centigrade, and the UK has its maximum rainfall. You can't go to the beach without a wetsuit and a flask of coffee before May and after August.

Nobody who's English has the faintest idea who St George was (and little idea what happened at the Battle of Trafalgar, or where it occurred), beyond the fact that St George killed a dragon (Why? When? Where? And why doesn't anyone ever point out that dragons don't exist?), and that Trafalgar involved Admiral Nelson. This is a pretty thin justification for an annual holiday: but that's not why we stage holidays, it appears. We do it so that people will stay in hotels.

I can't blame this entirely on the newspapers, but there are already plenty of special 'days' in our news. The purpose of declaring something an international day gives those committed to some cause or other the opportunity to celebrate together, and take strength from the cohesion of their community. At least that's the story. Once, this was probably true: for example on International Jesus Day (25 December).

Nowadays it's more useful as a way to get into the diary of a lazy journalist. There's a negligible chance that, if your job is publicising wombats, any newspaper will write anything about them. But, on 22 October every year, there's much more chance of a success, because it's their day. Not that the wombats care, as they celebrate the cohesion of their community by continuing to be wombats.

For example – for those of us united by having a Y chromosome – we celebrate International Men's Day in November. A card would be nice, thanks. I was surprised: what with being paid more to do the same job, possession of the TV remote and no requirement to wear high heels, every day is essentially Men's Day. Except for 8 March, of course, which is International Women's Day – which, despite being a holiday on half the planet, British men ignore every year. Maybe we're just doing the pretend-to-forget thing, like with anniversaries, birthdays and Valentine's Day.

Unaware of the correct way to celebrate International Men's Day, I checked on every ignorant journalist's go-to resource: Wikipedia. The entry from 2008 tells us only that 'University of Kent students celebrated International Men's Day at Mungo's Bistro on the university campus'. I can't imagine how I missed that item on the news.

Thanks to the vacant minds of some people in marketing departments globally, every day is basically International Something Day (ISD). Competition for ISDs is so intense that some are Trade Marked. Imagine if a rival band of angels decided to steal International Angel Day (TM) for example. On the other hand, you'd have thought that the angels among us would have been able to sort this out amicably.

The food business is a great creator of ISDs, because it encourages us to buy things to eat when we're fat and not hungry. If you like bacon, chefs, sushi, beer, pickles, waffles, picnics, cachaca, fruit or goats, there's an ISD for you. I'm not sure if you are meant to eat the goats or save them on International Goat Day, but take it from me: they're really tasty in a curry.

Causes love an ISD, and have grabbed special days for ozone, the poles (just one for both North and South), democracy, mountains, nurses, blondes, lighthouses, bogs, the dawn chorus and ponchos. Even jugglers have an ISD, which makes me want to slap them even more.

Like the nude charity calendar, ISDs have also become a joyless way to commercialise sex, so there are ISDs for whores, fetishes, kissing, orgasms... and firefighters.

And of course there's the niceness industry, equally divided between making us better people and the need to sell us things that exploit our self-loathing and consequent desperate desire to improve. For this try International Hug Day, or the ISDs for understanding and jokes or, for those who like to celebrate the truly meaningless, International Awareness Day.

Then if you are one of the few people in the world for whom a PR company has not created an ISD, why not simply piggy-back on someone else's. This, for example, is a real press release:

> In celebration of International Waffle Day, Radical Breeze is offering discounted packs of their software for MacOS X... 'Every year on March 25th, people around the world eat waffles. Lots and lots of waffles. Stacks of waffles,' stated Bryan Lund, president of Radical Breeze. 'This beautiful day must be commemorated. And what better way to do so than to offer stacks of great MacOS X software for a low price?'

Then there's the merely baffling. I'm hoping that the first International Accreditation Day (9 June: if the UK government tires of the St George idea and wants another holiday, civil servants would definitely get behind this one) will not be the last. Who could possibly miss the opportunity to take part in '[A] global initiative jointly established by the International Accreditation Forum (IAF) and International Laboratory Accreditation Cooperation (ILAC) to raise awareness of the importance of accreditation-related activities'.

Instead of this piecemeal approach, let's get organised and sell off the calendar properly, day by day. It would give the people who organised International Organisations Day something useful to do, and it might show us how important accreditation really is. We'd have to ring-fence important stuff like International Weblogger Day (oh yes, we have one too), but the others should just go to the highest bidder, no more than one day per group. Then we could stop messing around with greetings cards and parades and make some serious money out of celebrating the anniversary of nothing in particular by marketing 365 separate franchises and suing the hell out of each other. In this case every day would be International Lawyer's Day (currently limited to 5 April), but that's a small price to pay.

If you work in some brass instrument public relations capacity and you were the person who scheduled International Tuba Day for the first Friday in May because you were flat out of ideas and nobody cares about tubas, this might seem like bad news. In PR, one of the few reasons to create an ISD is that nobody owns the days of the year: your ISD may be pointless but it is very cheap, so clients like it as a publicity strategy.

Global capitalism solves this problem. A clever entrepreneur could pick up one of the cheaper days and resell it at an affordable price, moment by tedious moment, so 3 am to 4 am on 18 May can be International Kilt Hour, rather than the entire day it is given currently. Nobody wants to celebrate the kilt for an entire day, not even kilt manufacturers, and 3 am would be cheap enough for an industry with low margins. And for pointless imagination-free PR-driven celebrations of nothing (whoever came up with International Crochet Day, I'm talking to you[8]), two minutes a year ought to be more than enough.

Icon therefore I am

What have the Lollipop Person of the Year Competition and Lady Gaga's sunglasses got in common? Oh come on, it's not that hard. The answer is they are among the 26,000 things that have been described as 'iconic' in the press in the last three months.

Iconicity (iconicism? iconification?), my made-up word meaning 'the tendency to write that something is iconic because you can't be bothered to think of an accurate way to explain it', is up by a factor of about six since the millennium. Look at the graph of the use of the

Figure 3.5   Great news: stuff is on an iconicity uptick

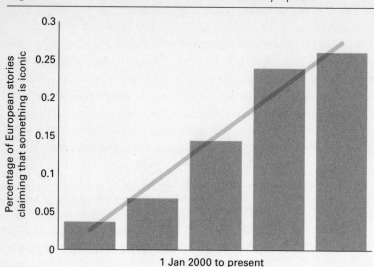

Percentage of European stories claiming that something is iconic

1 Jan 2000 to present

word in the European press, shown in Figure 3.5. The source, as ever, is Factiva.

(If you think I am unfairly targeting journalists because this is all down to over-caffeinated PR people, I think you're wrong. Of the 46,000-odd mentions of 'iconic' since the beginning of 2008, only 143 came from PR Newswire. This one's simply lazy journalism, it seems.)

I think some of the explosive growth comes from the need to write about inexplicably famous people who don't have an obvious talent. Calling their hair, their outfits or their body parts 'iconic' is handy when there's just nothing polite we can say.

Perhaps this is why, when I think of the word 'iconic', I often think of money and effluent. So I had a look to see how often the word is popping up in the accountancy press and among waste management writers, to see if my instincts are correct.

As you can see (Figure 3.6), after a slow start, much more of the accountancy trade has become iconic. The word is most often used in articles about cost reduction, the iconic financial strategy of recent years.

And the adjective is trending strongly in the waste management and sewerage sectors too (Figure 3.7).

Figure 3.6 Accountants: increasingly iconic too...

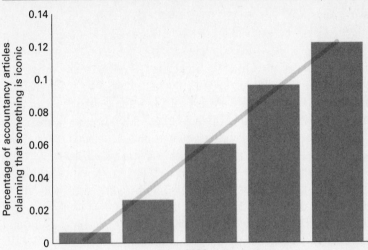

Figure 3.7 ... but then again, so is sewerage

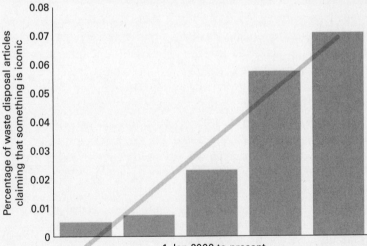

It also pleases me that, in this category, the word iconic comes up most often in articles about the stuff that the industry calls solid waste.

We've run out of things to write about

We're not short of news. Things keep happening, and we get the chance to see things happen all the time, because someone records it on a cameraphone, for example.

However, the number of news outlets has grown much faster, and that reduces the ability to explain, if not to report. And their business model has changed: there are a lot of stories that need to be written, but not much money to pay people to write them. Luckily, there are other people who take up the job, and public relations companies, often staffed by former journalists, have the required skill.

The examples of how the press is failing in its job to be an explainer: using idiotic pseudo-scientific formulae, attaching things to days of the year, describing things as iconic instead of telling us why they might be important or distinctive – are symptomatic as a trend towards having the story pre-packaged, like baby food.

Note: as a journalist, I'm not pretending to be above all this.

Chuckling at the fact that there is a feature in a free newspaper telling us that it is International Kilt Day because there's a picture of a celebrity in a kilt doing a pretend Scottish dance isn't a crime, it's just a bit depressing to see when your friends do it: it's like watching a village idiot laughing at a balloon on a stick. But we've always been like this. If anyone remembers 1970s British television, for example, the racier output involved carrots that viewers sent in because they approximated the shape of a penis.[9]

What's new is the industrialisation of lowest-common-denominator journalism. I'm not complaining about tabloid sensationalism: you might not like the big splash stories, but many of them are carefully researched and written, and some are genuinely important. I'm talking about the propagation of stories by cut-and-paste, known in the business as churnalism, a term coined by BBC journalist Waseem Zakir.[10]

Churnalism exposes the guilty secret that journalists have always copied ('lifted') stories from their competitors. Now it's much easier to do, because you have more sources. There are the news stories published on the internet, which can be searched using Google for the most part. There are press releases, which are e-mailed to us, and so we can simply search our e-mail inboxes instead of trying to file them. And, of course, there's Wikipedia.

The result is that the same story will be copied, often exaggerated, and distributed around the world. Very few of the 'writers' know anything about it, because they haven't spoken to anyone who had anything to do with it. They selectively reinterpret the limited (and possibly inaccurate – they don't know) information that they have.

Occasionally the results are funny: in 2009 Shane Fitzgerald, a sociology student at University College Dublin, planted a quote from composer Maurice Jarre in his Wikipedia page ('One could say my life itself has been one long soundtrack... When I die there will be a final waltz playing in my head, that only I can hear') which was plainly silly if you paused to think about it: it doesn't even make sense. But, when the composer died, British, Indian and Australian newspapers carried the quote in their obituaries.

It can also lead to a dull flattening of the language. Iconicity occurs partly because, once something has been anointed as 'iconic', it's easy for someone who is pressed for time to repeat it. This is not only safe (you didn't make it up, you copied it from someone else who said it), but it also enforces the iconicity of the icon – see, everyone's saying it.

We can criticise journalists for this, and rightly so, but the problem applies to all of us. When we write at work, we are all churnalists if we don't understand what we're writing about, and don't have the time or the will to find out. In this way, strange messages are distributed around a company, poorly understood and misused, repeated to customers and press and people unlucky enough to have wandered into your presentation when they were looking for the gents.

We don't all have the power to influence this. If the person from Sainsbury's who told me that 'We set very high standards for everything we sell', when I complained that a tin of beans had sliced my finger open because it was designed to be immune to the full arsenal of commercial can openers that I employed on it, wondered, as I did, what 'very high' means, and how the standards were set in this case because there was clearly a way in which the setting process was sub-optimal, they wouldn't be welcomed into the boss's office to discuss it.

On the other hand, many of us take in information and try to explain it to others. There are 156 million public blogs,[11] and far more pub gossip. Writing, telling and reading that information works better when we don't just repeat the last thing we heard.

The entertainers

News is only partly about new things: it is also entertainment, though often not entertainment to make us proud. We will only read the second sentence if we are excited by the first one, and that emotional connection can be exploited: prejudice, suspicion, hate, envy and anger are emotions too, and powerful ones. We worry about our safety, our families, our jobs and our money more than we worry about the safety, families, jobs and money of other people.

This isn't a bad thing. It can cure one of the problems of office communication: we're reading it, but we don't know why we've been given it to read. I note that a publisher for whom I wrote some semi-scholarly treatments of what philosophers had to say about business culture recently repacked my work as part of an anthology called MAKE MORE MONEY. I can't guarantee a result for you (if I could, why would I write a book about it?), but I think it will work for them.

Making money is entertaining: there's an argument that some people are motivated by the entertainment value. It's a powerful argument. 'House prices set to surge' was the *Daily Express* headline on 18 January 2011. It's exciting for homeowners, reporting that 29 per cent more surveyors thought that house prices would fall than thought they would rise. The difference the previous month had been 44 per cent, which is the origin of the headline.

You might consider this isn't entertainment as much as old-fashioned distortion, which is a venerable newspaper tradition. You would be correct. The *Express* is fitting the news to a bigger narrative: for many years it has reported the news through its effect on house prices, having decided that this is the barometer of happiness for its readers in a more powerful way than share prices, interest rates or any of the other factors that influence those prices, and this was the closest thing it could get to good news.

Meme me

Finding a powerful emotional trigger leads to stereotyping (the *Express* reader thinks primarily of house prices, for example), but from time to time we also decide on a single story, or simple idea, and go for it. Internet types call this a 'meme': fads, catchphrases, ways of thinking about a subject catch on, and quickly restrict our thinking to narrow, conventional wisdom.

Memes aren't necessarily wrong but they are often dull and obvious. I can't tell you how many times someone has told me in business that it's important to add value. Of course it is, it wouldn't be value unless it was important to add it. And yet this is emotionally satisfying enough to be an entire argument: I don't know what the value might be, or why it would be important, how important, or who would find it important. Memes grab attention: they stop us from talking normal.

Rooney, jazz or pork?

Here is an example of a meme from the world of sport, where the tribal, emotional nature of the activity means we tend to fit the facts to the opinion. The question under discussion in the UK before the 2010 World Cup: Was Wayne Rooney world class?

For those of you who don't like football this might seem a pointless, irrelevant or even irritating question. He'd do exactly the same thing on the pitch whether he was world class or not. But we're a class-based society. We need to know what class he is: it makes us feel comfortable.

It's not like sport, and football in particular, is in need of another measurement system – what with goals, wins, losses, draws, points, tournaments and cups. World classness, though, has two advantages: it can mean anything you want, and you can apply it to anything or anyone if you're lazy enough. It is a cross-sector measurement system which helps us to pat ourselves on the back in a non-specific way: if you describe yourself as world class on your website we might think you're a fantasist, but we can't take you to court for it. At least, not until I'm making the laws.

This is why our chunky hero's status is just one of many discussions of world-classness that occurs at any time: at the same time as what we must call the Rooney Debate was raging in the press, the world's media was also debating whether Miami is a world-class city, whether the UK's high-speed rail project was world class enough, and when ESI 'Expands Its Singapore-Based Operations to Support Its Asian Micromachining & Passive Components Customers' (I just report it, I don't necessarily understand it), does this enhance its position as a leading supplier of world-class photonic and laser systems? I'm sure you don't need me to tell you the answer to that one.

I once listened to a speech from a politician who spent 15 minutes explaining why London was not just a 'world city' but a 'world-class city'. He asked that we didn't interrupt with questions, no matter how anxious we were to ask them. He needn't have worried, to be honest.

As world-classness has become a de facto global ranking system for more or less everything on which we have opinions, I thought I'd make use of it. Before England departed for the World Cup in 2010, I Googled news for what was 'world class' that day and picked the first two non-sporting products I could find to compare to the Little Ginger Wizard: I hoped that I could tame a meme, and create information from entertainment. Using the comparison I hoped, pathetically, to get some kind of insight into Rooney's world-classness in a wider context. Which is why I am the only writer to give you an analysis of how Rooney's quality compares to jazz music and the US National Pork Board.

Like England's Great Hope, jazz music inspires strong emotions. Let us not forget that, in December 2009, an attendee at a jazz festival in Spain called the police when he heard Larry Ochs play.[12] But is jazz as a whole better or worse than Wayne Rooney? WE NEED TO KNOW.

And are both of them better than The National Pork Board – after all, pork is a controversial meat that has been dividing selectors' opinions ever since Deuteronomy didn't pick it all those years ago.

For Rooney, jazz and the Pork Board I divided the number of articles each year that claim world-classness by the number that didn't. First, the good news. Rooney was becoming more world class in the eyes of the, er, world (Figure 3.8).

But as you can see, opinion is volatile. Not so with jazz, which is consistently accorded world-class status far in excess of that of England's Pugnacious Goal Machine (Figure 3.9).

Jazz has shown staying power, but there are a lot of people claiming to be world class these days. Rooney might have been scoring at will, but in the run-up to the World Cup he's still not as consistently reported as being world class as The US National Pork Board, which has really hit form since 2008 (Figure 3.10).

Next time an England football fan tells you that 'I think we can win it this time, Rooney's world class',[13] just say to him that it's a good job

Figure 3.8   Rooney: maybe world class

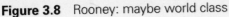
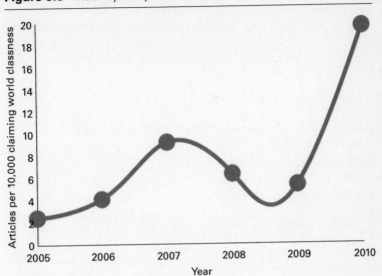

Figure 3.9   Jazz: consistently world class

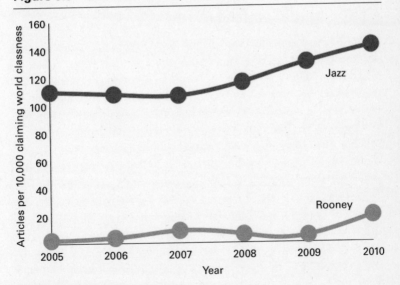

we were not playing the Game of Bacon against team USA in the World Cup on 12 June 2010, or we would have looked even worse. On the other hand, I reckon England could take them at jazz. That Larry Ochs is rubbish.

Figure 3.10   National Pork Board: running into form at the right time

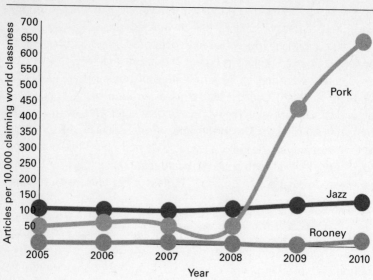

A tripe-hound on frog island

Astute Talknormalists among you will have discerned that, often, the word 'meme' is used as a weasel word for the more accurate description: 'prejudice'. If you're somehow emotionally, or financially, invested in the internet and social media, then it's inconvenient to find out that the packages of information and ideas that it distributes so efficiently are often just retreads of the old information and ideas that our culture has cherished lovingly for generations.

An example is the idea that an intelligent older woman must be a batty, lonely obsessive. Why did I pick this? Because at the end of 2009, Professor Christian Kay, the editor of the *Historical Thesaurus of the Oxford English Dictionary*, did a series of radio interviews. We have the interviews, and we have her polite and amused opinion too, which she posted in a blog[14] immediately afterwards.

Some background on Professor Kay: she is an expert on unusual historical words who has been compiling a book of them, on and off, for 44 years. She is softly spoken, unmarried and Scottish. This is a gift to any news programme with time to fill and lazy journalists.

It's a fascinating book, and an important historical document that shows how our language has evolved, but the coverage given to her efforts in 2009 – Google her name, you'll find it – owes more to those shows in which people sit in a bath of baked beans for a week. We're no longer comfortable talking about books and knowledge, but we know how to deal with harmless eccentrics.

In her blog she described the odd process of publicising an academic book to journalists (In the *Thesaurus*: *tripe-hounds*) who so desperately want her to be a caricature of herself: they wanted a bookish, Scottish, tweedy little old lady who is doing the literary equivalent of crocheting the world's longest scarf. One even went as far as to ask Professor Kay, the Honorary Professorial Research Fellow at the University of Glasgow, if she actually had a big piece of knitting to get back to: 'I'd like to put it on record that I do not have, and never have had, "a big piece of knitting" ', Professor Kay tells us. I am happy to assist in setting the record straight.

Instead she brings lists of strange words to interviews because that's what they're going to ask (*paddanieg*: an island with frogs on it). And like most women over 40 in the media she finds herself defined over and over again by her age. Her colleagues offered to give her a badge with 'I am 69' written on it 'to forestall such questions'.

Professor Kay seems to have handled the tedious sub-Miss-Jean-Brodie ageism and sexism cloaked as human interest with good humour. But she writes that she was nevertheless: 'startled that in 2009 a newspaper would produce a headline describing me as a "lingo-loving spinster", and one, moreover, who "coyly confessed" to celebrating publication with a glass of champagne'.

That was the *Daily Mail*, using what we shall politely call one of its little memes. So I guess she got off lightly: had she been an immigrant gay single parent and produced the same work, the coverage might not have been so indulgent.

Kate Middleton: common or commoner?

When I learned from the PA Newswire that 9 January 2011 had been Kate Middleton's last birthday as a commoner, I checked my watch. Sure enough, it wasn't the 16th century. It just sounded like it.

As an atheist who would prefer to live in a republic, let's just say I'm as excited by Royal weddings as I was by the visit of the pope. But it's a great example of how we entertain ourselves by creating stories to fit our mobile preconceptions.

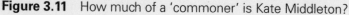

Figure 3.11   How much of a 'commoner' is Kate Middleton?

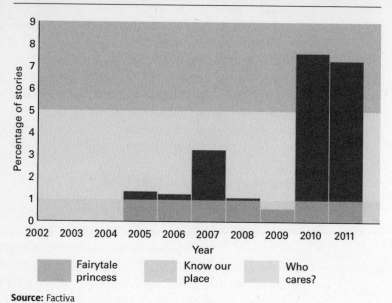

Source: Factiva

In an age when there's sadly less automatic respect for the ruling classes than in the past (for them, at least), I thought I'd check how often the former student of £22,000-a-year Marlborough College and future princess Kate was described in the British press as a commoner, in that Olde Englishe voice that we use to describe the exercise and systems of autocratic power, and how often the newspapers just come out and accuse her of being common – translation, having ideas above her station.

The branding of Kate Middleton as a 'commoner' began at the same time as the speculation about an engagement to Prince William, what with them having been going out together for a while and all (Figure 3.11). When Kate and Wills split up in 2007 – and as long as they stayed separate – it wasn't a useful description, because she wasn't so much a 'commoner' as a private citizen. They mean the same thing; it's just that one sounds extraordinary, and one's too boring to write about.

Then they got back together, and 'commoner' could be used to create a fairytale princess meme: the ordinary girl who won the heart of the handsome prince.

Figure 3.12 How 'common' is Kate Middleton?

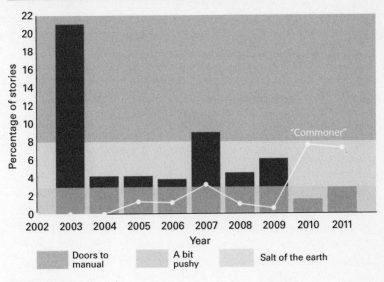

Source: Factiva

When you start this argument in the pub, people will tell you, often quite rudely, that being a commoner (breeding) isn't the same as being common (class). But, usefully, the press can swap one for the other and wink-wink signal the same thing. Kate and Wills are married now, so the royalist press have to stop insulting her parents for obviously being far too poor, but it wasn't always the case (Figure 3.12).

For example, this from the *Daily Telegraph*'s article 'Divided by family misfortunes' on 16 April 2007:

> Some of William's circle would even whisper 'doors to manual' when Miss Middleton arrived, in a jibe at her mother being a former airline stewardess.
> There were even worse social sins, such as using the word 'toilet' not 'lavatory', saying 'pleased to meet you' rather than 'how do you do?', and 'pardon' rather than 'what?'.

Imagine! The shame! And here's me obsessing about the trivial stuff.

It's not that the *Telegraph* agrees with this pathetic snobbery or anything, it's just saying, albeit with more relish than you'd expect.

When the press assumed that Kate was just William's bit of rough in 2003, almost one in four stories asked if she was common. Fast forward to the end of 2010: the description of her family as 'common' has been ruled out. People haven't changed their opinion (except people who base their opinion on the words used to describe people they don't know in newspapers), they just don't want to be rude to the Queen.

The socialisers

Committed Talknormalists everywhere are accustomed to viewing what's published in our newspapers with scepticism, and now we can delight in the comments sections of online newspapers too, where people who might have first-hand knowledge of the story, for example, or an expert opinion, or just a relevant criticism of bias will post their point of view.

So also with blog culture, in which the post is simply the first part of a conversation between poster and readers. It's not like buying a paperback book, where you'd have to e-mail the author[15] if you disagreed with him, and then everyone else who'd read the book too, just to warn them.

That's how it is supposed to work. Blogging should be a process of Talknormalisation, by definition: if there weren't blogs, there wouldn't have been one called Talk Normal. If there's a bigger picture, then you are not limited in what you hear by the interests of people who own the means of distribution. The people can speak, and you can choose who you listen to.

So what's the problem? Simply put: while the means to publish has been democratised, there's less progress on access to information. What you write about something depends on what you know about it. What others write about it depends on what they know.

There are two restrictions on what you know: what you can find out, and who you choose to listen to.

There are no restrictions on who you choose to listen to, except the ones you put on yourself. Social media can be a force for Talknormalisation, but it can also be a pure engine for what scientists call 'choice shift'.

The concept is simple, universal and consistent: MIT student James Stoner discovered it – or at least was the first to write about it formally – in 1961. When a group discusses a subject, it adopts a more extreme position on that subject than individuals who have not participated in a discussion. Prejudiced individuals become more prejudiced, political views become more extreme.

This isn't what we expect. The main point of holding meetings, especially since companies started to remove the biscuits, is to stop some loose cannon doing something crazy. If a group (battery?) of loose cannons get together, it implies they might do something that even they would have individually decided was wacky. This might, for example, explain Harley-Davidson's decision to launch a perfume and range of wine coolers.[16]

This sometimes makes social media function in the opposite way to which idealists would like it to function: instead of synthesising an informed consensus, we pick the blogs we like because they represent our views – which may be informed, or may be prejudices based on ignorance. We read stuff we like to hear, and we participate in a group discussion, which strengthens our point of view.

In the place where people who disagree gather, there are equally committed social media users travelling in the opposite direction. The loyal readers of a blog called Talk Abnormal are not going to come round to our point of view any time soon. I haven't received any threats yet, but I know it's just a matter of time.

When social and traditional media mix, the result can be anything but the improvement that lazy thinking implies. And when communities decide how exciting something is, and those communities then publish their excitement, social media is little more than an echo chamber.

Citizen journalism: not always A Good Thing

The November 2009 *Atlantic Monthly* magazine published a carefully researched article called 'The Story Behind the Story'[17] by veteran journalist Mark Bowden (he wrote *Black Hawk Down*, among other things) about how social media, and citizen journalism in particular, can skew lazy traditional media.

His argument: the collapse of the business model for traditional journalism means that the quest for information has been superseded by the quest for ammunition. His case study was the confirmation hearing for Judge Sonia Sotomayor, who had been nominated to the Supreme Court (and who was confirmed after the hearings).

An odd thing happened when she was nominated: immediately all the TV networks used the same package of video of her seeming to make extremist comments, a major news story which undermined her credibility. In the article, Bowden tracks down the blogger who unearthed the videos – and the advocacy groups that disseminated them.

On the face of it, 'Blogger does the legwork that journalists don't and gets a story' is a good-news story about internet culture. Anyone who complains about citizen journalists doing their job must be a bitter old-school journalist, you think.

I say: not so. Bowden makes two points:

1 When journalists do not have the time or the skills, someone else will step in to provide ready-made stories. The lack of resource in journalism means these stories go straight on to the page or the screen, and so are effectively endorsed by the publication.

2 The people who do it have their own agenda: 'Work formerly done by reporters and producers is now routinely performed by political operatives and amateur ideologues of one stripe or another, whose goal is not to educate the public but to win. This is a trend not likely to change', as Bowden puts it.

And that's the important difference. Most citizen journalists, advocacy groups and public relations companies are not motivated by the desire to get to the truth, but to deliver a point of view. No problem: it's their job to work backwards from a conclusion (or, for citizen journalists, it is their vocation, because there's no money in it). It is the job of the reporter to check whether that conclusion has any value.

And so professional journalists must take some responsibility: in this case, and many others, they have not done their job. For years journalists (I'm part of the problem here) have been pleased to have stories fed to us, complete with partial research, friendly quotes and conclusions. We can't suddenly complain when we realise that it has made us into the advocacy industry's gimps. Now, thanks to forces beyond our control, many newspapers, news stations and magazines are no longer set up to check the stories they report.

Judge Sotomayor was confirmed, but the damaging news clips of her led on every major news station. In his feature Bowden checked the context and discovered that the clips, far from being the secret confession of a deranged idealogue, contained little of interest and nothing new. That is, until they were taken out of context by a politically motivated blogger and presented to the media, who didn't bother to check them.

If you're in the business of winning approval for your clients, this is good news. But in the long term this culture of advocacy is dangerous. We no longer have any idea who is shaping the news at any level, and as citizens we can never know enough to separate good research from carefully disguised bias when we watch or read the news. Bowden concludes about this type of media that: 'Today it is rapidly replacing journalism, leading us toward a world where all information is spun, and where all "news" is unapologetically propaganda.'

When that happens, ultimately we all lose.

What do you play WoM with?

I'm delighted that the internet industry buzzword 'viral' is now often replaced with the much more Talknormal 'word of mouth', even if the word isn't coming from a mouth. I'm less excited to see it has now become an acronym: 'WoM'. And I'm positively unpsyched to hear that this has spawned a WoM industry, which contains WoM agencies who use WoM marketing to achieve WoM goals. It's hard to type when your hands are clenched in fists of rage, but I must continue.

As with many of these functions, there's a side that's pure business, and there's a side which all of us who care about truth and authenticity should deplore.

McKinsey calculates that 67 per cent of consumers base their purchase decisions primarily on WoM. It's the most reliable source of information according to 93 per cent of consumers, NOP tells us. It's the fastest-growing area of marketing.

In his book *OBD: Obsessive Brand Disorder* (Public Affairs, 2009), Lucas Conley says that WoM activity is $3.7 billion of the investment of brands such as Coca-Cola and P&G in their branding. That's still just over 1 per cent of the money carefully apportioned and invested, or alternatively pointlessly wasted, on the obsessive rebranding by which we now mark the passing of time in the marketing business, but the other bit isn't our problem right now.

P&G is particularly good at WoM. It has recruited 250,000 teens (1 per cent) and 600,000 moms (7 per cent of the mom population), and charges other brands to have access to them. The brands send product, and the recipients are encouraged to try the brands out and tell their friends about them.

A bit creepy, you might think, but hardly criminal. On the other hand, the coordinated efforts to usurp social media using fake positive or negative reviews, for example, are a crime against Talknormalism.

Exhibit 1 for this: TripAdvisor. If you've ever used this consumer recommendation site when you are planning a holiday, it's an excellent way to save money. First because you can compare prices on your hotel, and second because, when you read the negative reviews that your chosen hotel has attracted from one of the other 11 million users of the site, you prefer to stay at home.

In 2011, a group of 420 hoteliers accused TripAdvisor of failing to weed out fake reviews posted by other hotels as part of a scorched-earth marketing strategy: many had checked their records for evidence of the guest who had posted the worst reviews, and found that the guest, surprise, hadn't actually stayed there.

TripAdvisor claims this isn't a problem, and that it flags suspicious reviews.

We might argue that, if hoteliers are so determined to form a circular firing squad, we should just let them get on with it. But it isn't just hoteliers. In 2010, the US Federal Trade Commission announced that PR company Reverb Communications settled charges of deceptive advertising: interns posted 'independent' reviews of apps by the firm's clients on iTunes. The company was forced to remove all its fake posts. Its clients include Harmonix, which published Rock Band 3, and some of Apple's most successful apps developers.

Way to go, interns! At least it means they were learning useful business skills: how to pretend you like something that's obviously a terrible idea; how to do what your boss tells you to do; how to use social media at work. And it's more creative than spending a month doing the photocopying and fetching coffee for no pay.

So is WoM positive or negative for Talknormalists? That's like asking whether social media in general is good or bad. It means that companies who make dud products can't pretend that everything is OK: it doesn't matter what the deputy marketing manager tells journalists, a hundred one-star reviews on Amazon exposes the lie – unless, of course, the manufacturer's competition employs some very hard-working interns.

The War on Hyberbole

We're at war. I'm sure you noticed.

There are the usual military wars but, for people who like to call talk radio stations at 4 am or visit their golf club bar to complain, the real wars are closer to home.

For example, if you're the type of person who, before forming an opinion, wonders 'What would Jeremy Clarkson think?' you will have noticed that there is a War on Motorists going on.[18] Don't worry, car fans. I live two minutes from the A12, and I can tell you that you've already won this one. My advice to militant motorists: rather than whining about speed cameras and fuel tax and congestion charges and cycle lanes and car parking charges in the letters pages of local newspapers, open up a second front. Tarmac over the Eurostar line and invade France. Just as long as you promise not to come back.

The *Daily Mail* tells us that the government is busy recruiting ex-ministers for a War on Dole Cheats. I approve of less thieving, but Labour ex-ministers of all people should know that it's easier to start a war than to win one. Note also that Dole Cheats have been abusing the well-intentioned Tanks for the Homeless scheme for so long that they're armed and ready to fight for what isn't actually theirs. Well, they would be, but *The Jeremy Kyle Show* is on in half an hour, and after that the chippy's open.

A quick scan through one day's news also shows that there are wars of varying believability being waged on our behalf on antibiotics, cybercrime, gold, de-legitimisation, and media centre software. It's not an exaggeration, because they are exactly like real wars! If someone has to die so that media centre software can be defeated, one day our kids will thank us.

Also in the news: Lance Armstrong has declared war on the French hotel industry. Either that or he complained about some French hotels; but that doesn't sound quite as exciting when you're writing a headline.

This is a perfect example of the media's talent to exaggerate. Social media picks this ball up and runs with it. No, it sprints, faster than the speed of light!

Among blogger armchair generals you're never more than a couple of posts away from a fictitious War on Something. For example, over at loopy United Liberty, the dastardly US government is waging a War on Dogs,[19] in which we must take sides: 'A world where drugs are widely available legally would be supremely preferable to a world in which I have to fear that a SWAT team will break down my door and kill my pets', it concludes. I'm curious to see half a dozen sausage dogs in camouflage jackets trying to load a mortar, but I can't say I'm rooting for either side, based on this article.

You could say – wait for it – that I don't have a dog in this fight.

With everyone – and now their pets – currently conscripted in some media-invented war or other, our armed forces are going to be overstretched. I have a way to cut the workload: we can beat the internet's lazy writers at their own game by declaring a War on Hyberbole.

There may be a million-strong Blogger Army against us, doubt-lessly even now claiming they would die typing for the right to ex-aggerate, but I've got a plan to win that can't fail.

We wait for one of the Blogger Army to announce that he or she is the General. Ten comments later the rest of them will be far too busy – complaining that this blogger is doing exactly what Hitler would have done – to fight against us.[20]

Talknormalise me

We're all writers: not everyone has a novel in them, but we've all got a lot of e-mails to write. Every e-mail doesn't have to be a work of literature, but if you can't be understood, you wasted your time, and you're wasting the time that your readers give to reading your output.

What can you do? It's easier to spot the mistakes that other people make than diagnose your own errors. But the way to Talknormality is to improve your own work. Then, when you are accustomed to knocking your own words into shape, it's easier to find the problems that other people are experiencing, and fix those (or at least suggest a way in which they might be fixed: having edited other people's work for 20 years, criticising their work is a little like telling them that they have an ugly baby).

Editing yourself

The most important point about this: the mechanics are easier than you think they are. You need to have the confidence to cut entire paragraphs, not just to fiddle with the odd word. By this I mean that word processors and content delivery systems and e-mail editors have made it possible to change anything. In the days of the type-writer, you had to type a draft, mark it up with a pencil, and retype it. This was enormously tedious, but it taught the journalists who grew up with typewriters great clarity of thought. Working from sketchy notes, in a hurry, they could produce a good draft in a matter of minutes.[21]

Today we tend to assemble our documents, bit by bit. This section was originally in a completely different bit of the book. When I saw it made no sense, I cut and pasted it here. That gave me the chance to introduce this paragraph, but it meant deleting a similar paragraph which was originally on the next page.

Whether we produce a workable fist draft or fumble in the dark to assemble one, writing clearly is a skill, not a talent: meaning that it can be taught. We're not all going to be good at it, but it's an open secret that many great writers produce awful first drafts.

It's a rare skill to quickly assess what needs to be said, and to say it with discipline, make sure that it is easy to understand, no longer than it should be, and also that it is interesting.

Intuition is important. When it doesn't seem right, trust your gut.

Here's an example. This was published in *The Observer*, where football fans get to write about their own teams after they watched them:

> I'm very heartbroken after that performance. It's another game in which we have played well and not got a result – it's quite annoying in a way. However, saying that, when you go to Man Utd you do not generally expect to get too much. It just seems to be those lapses in concentration during the closing stages that are letting us down, which is frustrating. But everyone played well, particularly Stearman, and if we continue the way we played today I think we'll finish comfortably mid-table come the end of the season. Mick McCarthy just needs to keep the players positive.

Being 'very heartbroken' is the same as being 'heartbroken' – something is either broken or not. We know it's after the performance, because that's the point of the report. Saying that something is 'quite annoying in a way' is the same as saying it is 'annoying'. 'It just seems to be' isn't needed, not is 'which is frustrating', which adds nothing. 'But' isn't needed either. If you add that you will 'finish', you don't need 'come the end of the season'. McCarthy doesn't 'just' need to keep the players positive – there's a lot more to his job than that.

I'd argue that a first sentence that reads 'I'm heartbroken. It's annoying because we played well again and didn't get a result' has more impact, but you only see that because you take words that aren't needed away.

You can do this on almost any piece of writing. I dare say there's plenty of Talk Normal that could be pruned in this way, and would be improved as a result.

Picking a puppy

When I am allowed to train people, I teach them not to leave me with a list of three things, five things or ten things (that's PowerPoint thinking, which encourages us to produce lists) but to tell me what is the most important thing for our readers.

I call this 'picking a favourite puppy'. Imagine you are a child, and your parents put a basket of puppies on the table. 'Pick your favourite', they tell you.

'Why?' you ask, looking at the little furry things flopping around, biting your finger.

'Because we're going to drown the rest', they say. My methods are not to everyone's tastes.

My point? That someone has to pick what's memorable, the thing that they remember from what you've written. Newspapers write a headline, but just one. Even an e-mail has a subject.

Our short-term memory is not sophisticated. It holds one thing at any time – too many pieces of information bouncing around, and we are unable to concentrate. But you have many things to communicate to me at any time: many puppies, if you like.

But in any list, one thing is most relevant, important or urgent. If you are writing for me, then either you pick which one it is, or I will, but that choice will be made.

Blogging allows you to post two 400-word pieces that raise two straightforward points in two days, rather than a rambling 1,000-word piece that discusses a long list of barely connected facts. It would be foolish not to take advantage.

How do you know which puppy is best? There is no single answer. Think about the audience: What's most urgent for the readers? What is most likely to get the reaction you need? What is the subject that links the things you want to say?

Talknormalists rarely copy politicians, for obvious reasons, but when Bill Clinton wanted to become president of the United States, his strategist James Carville hung a sign on his wall: it said 'The Economy, Stupid'. He picked a puppy. The correct one, as it turns out: while his rival George H W Bush was a popular president – with 90 per cent approval in March 1991 – by the election most disapproved of his performance. They had been constantly reminded that the United States had been stuck in a recession by a campaign that had a focus.

Note: this doesn't mean ignoring everything else. There's more than one way to treat a topic, and I'm just suggesting that, if you genuinely believe that something is the most important puppy at that time, learn to discuss other things in how they relate to this puppy.

For example, Talk Normal is about many things: lies, waffle, jargon, what it's like to work in an office, statistics, media distortions, crazy bosses... this is getting us nowhere.

Start again: Talk Normal shows us how words are used to manipulate us. Jargon is used to exclude us and cover lies, our work uses words to create a cult-like atmosphere, the media chooses its words and stats selectively to influence the conclusions we reach. If we want more honesty and integrity in our relationships, that change starts with the way we describe the world around us. That's the most important thing Talk Normal can do.

The first attempt was like a bad PowerPoint presentation – a list of things. In the second paragraph it's all in there: just in a different order, which is easier to understand because it has a focus.

Clear thinking means better writing

Tim Radford was formerly *The Guardian*'s science editor, letters editor, arts editor and literary editor. My former editor at *The Guardian* told me that if I wanted to improve, I should write more like him, which I resented keenly at the time, even though it was entirely correct. Tim also composed 'A manifesto for the simple scribe', a set of 25 commandments for would-be journalists who wanted to improve their writing. This set of instructions has been doing the rounds for about 15 years[22] in newsrooms, but I wanted to find out how we could apply them to the day-to-day work of writing e-mails, reports, letters and all the documents that I receive, but don't understand or can't be bothered to finish.

So I asked Tim (TR below) to pretend that I was an idiot and a terrible writer, which he managed with polite aplomb. Maybe he had noticed my work all those years ago, and was just remembering his earlier emotions.

ME: I know it's a mess, but I don't know how to fix it. I've been fiddling with the text for a while, but it doesn't seem to get any clearer.

TR: First, just tell me what you want to say. The title or the subject is a good clue as to the question you should answer. You should be able to sum up what you're writing about in one sentence – and that's your first sentence. I used to think this was a rule for journalism, but it isn't. It's a rule for everything.

ME: I've boiled it down to half a dozen bullet points, if that helps?

TR: In which case you shouldn't be writing about it yet. The requirement is that you have to think about the thing first, until you know what the most important thing is. Don't start writing about it because you think you've got it, because you probably haven't.

ME: But it's complicated. There are so many things I want to include; they're all mixed up.

TR: Then find the most important, and leave out the rest if you can. Your writing is always simpler to understand if it is shorter and more direct, and that's the best way to say it. That's a special problem. Read too much, then write too much, and you end up with stuff that is extraneous. It is not worthless, but how do you say what you want in one sentence if you have all this extra stuff in there with it?

ME: I'm worried people will think I am stupid.

TR: This is not dumbing down. You are not over-simplifying. It's making something easier for everyone to understand. If you really want to know what good writing is like, pick up a book by George Orwell. He had a way of writing so that it seems like he is talking to you, but he writes about complicated ideas. No one accused Orwell of dumbing down.

ME: I've fixed the first sentence. It's the most important thing, and it tells people what I'm going to write. What next?

TR: The second sentence.

ME: This could be a long workshop.

TR: The first sentence is important because it makes people read the second sentence and it means they don't ignore what you have to say. If you have a really good story to tell, the second sentence just writes itself.

ME: Mine doesn't. I've got half a dozen second sentences.

TR: Then you are losing your train of thought. If you have to do a sales presentation, for example, the unspoken message is 'buy the bloody product'. Anything that doesn't add to that is a distraction. It's amazing how easily writers get distracted. I look at people reading a newspaper on public transport. They read the first paragraph, the second, maybe sometimes the third. If you haven't told them what they need to know at that point, you've wasted your time.

ME: I guess I can shove the other stuff down the bottom somewhere. In that case, what's the best length to write?

TR: About 25 per cent shorter than whatever you just wrote is a good rule of thumb. Newspaper journalists see a third or more of what they write thrown away by the subs. But the Gettysburg Address was 256 words long. If that was possible, most of what you need to express can be done tersely as well.

ME: But it's interesting. They should be interested too.

TR: No. We did an experiment years ago at *The Guardian*, and we asked 1,000 readers to sit down with a pencil and mark what they read. There was one story that nobody in our entire readership read that day: it was about economic reform in Suriname. It was very interesting to the person who wrote it, but we need the ability to step outside ourselves, and realise that there is no reason why anyone in the world should read what we just wrote, unless we give our audience a reason why it is important to them. For example, there's no incentive to read about a scientific discovery unless you think it might do something for you.

ME: So I need to solve their problem, or at least tell them what it is. But I get a bit lost halfway through, and I end up writing stuff that's not really going anywhere.

TR: You must keep the energy high, so that you are thinking about what you mean. It stops you writing cliché. The only thing that should 'hit the buffers' is something to do with railways. When we write 'at the end of the day', we're never talking about something that happens at the end of a day. We don't quite understand what we are saying, but we say it anyway because that's easier.

ME: But how do I know I've done a good job?

TR: It's always a good idea to have someone else read what you wrote, even if it's only your partner. When you communicate it is your job to say something that is clear and wonderful, and that other people wouldn't have been able to guess, and you need someone who will tell you if you failed.

Good communication is difficult

On the other hand, it's interesting, and it's a lot better for everyone than the alternative. My instruction from Tim Radford clearly brought out some important points that are worth incorporating into our search for Talknormalism:

1 There can be only one. Every piece of communication is about one thing above all others, and you need to find it. There are no newspaper articles with the headline: 'A list of the various things that a government might need to do and the possible outcomes', though the *New York Times* used to have some that ran it pretty close. Don't give lists unless there's a big reason why the list exists. Say that first.

2 The problem implies the solution. Why are you telling me this? There has to be a problem that needs to be solved. If this document didn't exist, we'd need to create it. If I know that, I'll read it.

3 Don't be afraid to be brutal. You'll get another chance next week to write another one of these. Save the subsidiary information for that document, cut it out.

4 Prioritise: accept they won't finish the document. Get the important stuff in first, like telling a joke backwards. If you build up to the punchline, your readers will have left.

5 Get outside help. We started this section with an explanation as to why sub-editors are useful. We all have our own internal editor – all except those people whom you tend to stay away from because they overshare compulsively – but it's even better to have someone who can be your editor. Maybe you can edit each other. But don't pick editors because they work for you, or anyone who feels obliged to be polite. Approval is the enemy of good style.

6 Finally, use your criticism. If someone says it's boring, don't tell them they're wrong, make it more interesting. If they point out that the important first sentence is in paragraph five, cut it and paste it to the top, rather than justifying the tedious first four paragraphs. Acting decisively to change what you do needs humility, but humility and Talknormalism go hand-in-hand.

Notes

1 Both quotes taken from *Flat Earth News* by Nick Davies, which is a must-read for all Talknormalists.
2 Next generation, flexible, robust, world class, scalable, easy to use, cutting edge.
3 http://bit.ly/gobgook
4 http://bit.ly/badform
5 I should note that Dr Carr disagrees with my characterisation of her strategy. I should make clear that I consider her work extremely valuable. The publicist's strategy, on the other hand, I hate.
6 For the statistical non-specialists, a non-random sample often makes data hard to draw conclusions from. If you made a survey of average earnings by going to the park and asking people who were asleep on a bench what they earned, it would be below the national average. Also a strong correlation suggests that A changes when B changes, and leaves open the possibility that change in A might possibly cause B (or B causes A, or they're both caused by C). A weak correlation means that B moves a little bit when A moves. It simply says that you can't rule out the possibility that A helps to cause B. However, Blythman assumes, making two errors, that A causes B on this basis.
7 Marchioness and countess, respectively. Pointless as it is, the second one's good for pub quizzes.
8 For crochet fans who e-mailed me, I'd like to point out: I've got nothing against your hobby. If I had to celebrate it for a whole day though, then I'd have to take a more robust stance.
9 This might not be true, but it's how I remember it.
10 How do I know this? I cut and pasted it from churnalism.com, a website created by the Media Standards Trust. See how easy it is?

11   Got that from Wikipedia too, so it might have been made up by a student.

12   I recommend you seek him out on YouTube. Ochs is the perfect example of a jazz musician that inspires a select few, and makes the rest of the world want to have him arrested.

13   Since I did this research, it has become much less likely that you'll hear this said by anyone at all. Sentiment on pork, meanwhile, seems broadly unchanged. It seems that Rooney had form (temporary) and pork has class (permanent).

14   Here: http://bit.ly/tripehound

15   tim@talknormal.co.uk

16   *Brand Failures* by Matt Haig (Kogan Page, 2003) has the story.

17   http://bit.ly/TNcitizens

18   On 13 May 2010 the government's Transport Secretary, Philip Hammond, promised to end the state's War on Motorists, bringing this secret – and completely made-up – war to a close, and winning cynical, cheap, approving headlines too.

19   Find the posting at http://bit.ly/warondogs, but don't let the government see you reading it.

20   And for once in their lives, they'd be correct.

21   The bible of how to do this is the wonderful book *Essential English for Journalists, Editors and Writers*, written by Harold Evans, published many times in many formats. Lots of people own it, but many think that purchasing it is the end of the process, rather like a gym membership.

22   You can find them here: http://bit.ly/simplescribe.

4 Tell and sell

Buy More S**t or We're All F***ked[1]

People twist words to make us buy their stuff. This is not news.

There's a fair chance, based on the mail and comments that I get at Talk Normal, that you're in the business already. Many of us are. Buying stuff is a patriotic duty: the UK and US governments urged us back to the shops in 2001 after 9/11, and in 2008 after the financial crisis.

George W Bush even appeared in an airline commercial while he was still president, urging people to start flying again, and ignore their fear of terrorism. He might not have been much of a president, but he could do for airlines what President Nixon couldn't do for used cars.

Our economy needs to grow. You could argue that the only difference between us and our ancestors, who stood on top of mounds covered in woad, is that we know how to market things to each other. It would be a ridiculous argument, but it sounds good, and so it is right at home in this section.

The gobbledygook machine

For those of you who listen to *Desert Island Discs*, you'll know that when the celebrities go to their imaginary desert island, they are

Figure 4.1   A briefing book

allowed to take the Bible plus one other book. It's only a matter of time until someone chooses their corporate briefing book.

If you don't know what a briefing book looks like, I created one for you (Figure 4.1).

It's one thing for the prime minister to have a big book with details of everything from knife crime crackdowns to puffin colonies with him at prime minister's questions. It's his job to know everything, but his head would burst like a ripe watermelon if he had to keep it all in there. Might be fun to try, though.

Our current predicament is another thing entirely: a corporate culture in which a product manager is unable to speak without reading the lines from a company's messaging document.

I once believed that the messaging document is the greatest enemy of Talknormalism in the world of marketing. Obviously, I realise there are greater dangers. A messaging document can't kill you – though I've seen plenty that would break your foot if you dropped them.

I don't believe they should all be burned in the metaphorical town square. I'll even concede that companies have to have consistent messages, and a way to send those out to people who often have no more idea of what their employer actually makes than they have of what's down the back of their sofa, and so might confuse the two, with hilarious results.

The problem isn't the idea of the document, but what's done with it.

First, communications departments keen to justify their existence bloat the document on the assumption that 50 pages of advice is better than 5 pages, offering an answer for every question and a mantra for every situation. If you have gone to this trouble, it often follows that everyone should follow the document to the letter.

But compiling a big document by committee – which is how it's done – means it's very difficult to say anything of value. As soon as you do, someone's going to edit it. If you're contributing to one of these, it's not in your interest to stick your neck out.

Sadly, some journalists are focused entirely on performing interviews by e-mail, allowing the guardians of the book to simply cut and paste dull answers into the reply, attributing it to some director or other, without going to the hassle of even consulting them.

The result? A growth in the number of spokespeople who are corporate speak-your-weight machines. And some who don't even know what has been said in their name.

The worst press release in history, and how I found it

The basis of communication with the general public has, for many years, been the press release. They lay out what companies are doing, and give phone numbers and e-mail addresses so that journalists can call and say, 'I saw your press release, I didn't read it, what does it say?' Journalists are impatient that way.

This means that press releases are subject to two disciplines designed to make them less normal: they are compiled by committee, because all sorts of people think they know best, so they get longer and less easy to understand. They are also compiled by people who want to show off, so information alone doesn't cut it. We need to be told what to think about the information, and that creates a breathless excitement over contract wins and partner relationships and value-added services and looking forward and all sorts of ideas that demand to be liked.

Reading a pile of press releases is like being licked by a needy, slightly smelly dog.

As a man of science, I wanted to find the worst press release in history. It stands to reason there must be a worst press release, and it would be useful to use it to frighten our children, just like my boarding school used to make us eat spam fritters once a week to teach us how to hide spam in our pockets. At least, that's what I learned.

Luckily, I'm not the only person who snoops around in Factiva looking for bad communication to make fun of. When I was writing about how newspapers weed out jargon – or not, in the UK, where journalists wave it through to make the rest of us unhappy, I referenced the work of David Meerman Scott, who established a list of the most overused rubbish gobbledygook phrases in the language, and did some entertaining analysis on them.

At this point, I pick up his torch.

In order, Meerman Scott's top 10 worst offenders were: next generation, flexible, robust, world class, scalable, easy to use, cutting edge, well positioned, mission critical and market leading. I'm sure I've listened to keynotes where all of them came in a single sentence, but it takes some nerve to commit more than two or three of them to a single press release and then let other people see it.

I wanted to find the release that used the most of them. When I searched PR Newswire on Factiva I imposed one rule: I looked for single releases that were 2,000 words or less to exclude the 'mega press pack' effect – because, like with an infinite number of monkeys, if you leave enough press release writers in front of a computer for long enough, then combine their output together in a single giant release that describes a really rubbish trade show (for example), it might have every piece of drivel ever conceived in it.

Imagine a release like that! Well, I've witnessed one, and let me tell you: it's like staring at the sun – but not in a good way.

First of all I searched Factiva, the giant archive of magazine and newspaper articles and press releases, for the press releases using the worst phrase as chosen by Scott's panel ('next generation'), then searched inside that category for the number of releases with the worst two jargon phrases used together, and so on.

Until the end of 2009 there had been more than 77,000 releases in history which talk about next generation something-or-other, with Factiva reporting that the top five offenders were Microsoft, Motorola, Lucent, Sun and Texas Instruments.

Add 'flexibility', and the number drops to less than 9,000, but – get this – the same five companies are the five most frequent transgressors.

At this point we note that, from now on, no one outside of the technology business even gets into the top 10. More of that in a minute.

Add another term ('robust'), and we're down to around 150 releases per year. Lucent temporarily drops out of the power five, and in comes Intel. Only one in ten of these releases – barely more than one per month at this stage – adds the claim of 'world classness' to this potent mix. Intel's gone, Lucent is back, and in a move that will be satisfying to many in the Unix community (techie joke), Sun is suddenly gobbledygook provider number one, ahead of Microsoft! It couldn't win the technology war, but when it comes to the battle to put the four most overused c**p phrases into a press release most often, Sun finally bests its bitter rival. Factiva tells me Sun also had the largest share of the 60-odd releases in history that have included 'scalability' with the other four jargon phrases.

Eliminate every press release that carelessly fails to mention 'easy to use', and we're down to six releases in 10 years. Could anyone use *every one* of the top seven gobbledygook terms in one press release? Sun falls at the final hurdle and is beaten by Lucent, the only company in history that dared to add 'cutting edge' to the other six phrases and was shameless enough to send the release out.

When, in 2006, Lucent announced that 'Six New European Value Added Distributors Contract to Resell Lucent's Security Portfolio',[2] the press office probably had no idea that this was the high-water mark in the tsunami of twaddle that we experienced in the noughties. Ms Martina Gruger-Buhs and Mr Peter Benedict, your names were on the document; but something tells me this was a collaborative effort.

Commiserations to Sun Microsystems too: no one could have tried harder to give me a headache.

I'd hate to see the bad stuff

I thought it was about time that Talk Normal sent out its own press release. I don't have anything to talk about, but that hasn't stopped PR companies from sending me thousands of press releases in the past, so look at this as part of some ineffective passive-aggressive retaliation.

Anyway, having received almost half a million press releases in my life, I gave the project several seconds of thought before coming up with:

Talk Normal expands Solution Portfolio with new Solution Modules

Talk Normal (**http://talknormal.co.uk**), the leading website for people who want to communicate more effectively with coworkers, today announces the Talk Normal Interaction Effectiveness Solution. The solution consists of a series of discrete modules which together effectively enhance your ability to provide effective interactions end-to-end in your business, and facilitate improved interaction.

'Talk Normal has always set out to be significantly customer-focused,' chief solution advocate Tim Phillips says, 'with our solution we can take this to another level.'

The solution is free to view by visiting **http://bit.ly/124lr**, and is available immediately.

###

About Talk Normal

Talk Normal (**http://talknormal.co.uk**) is the leading website for people who want to communicate more effectively with coworkers. Its chief solution advocate is Tim Phillips.

Contact

Tim Phillips, chief solution advocate

tim@talknormal.co.uk

020 xxx xxxx

I thought, maybe someone who does this for a living could tell me what you think of my style (with hindsight I could have punched up the bit where I called it a website. Information portal? Content repository?) but luckily there's a free website to tell me how effective my release would be as a marketing tool: **http://pressrelease.grader.com**. You paste your release and the robot at HubSpot, which runs it, automatically writes you a report.

My report told me that I need to vary the links a bit more for search engine optimisation and my press release should be at least twice as long, as I'm sure you agree. But it's not all bad news: the report told me that 'This release contains 0 words that are considered gobbledygook'.

I support anything that gives us better press releases, especially as so many of them reach the pages of magazines virtually untouched these days. But if the HubSpot robot is interfacing with my information portal, and it genuinely wants to facilitate improved interaction, I'd suggest tightening that gobbledygook filter a bit.

Happy talking

It's important we feel good: we've dealt with this before in the section on Newspeak. The closer we look at the language used to sell us things, the more we can see the fixed grin of people trying to make us happy about what we're doing.

It may be the common shared activity of commerce: when your job is to persuade us to spend time we can't spare to buy things we don't need with money we don't have, you've got to sugar coat it a bit.

I'm really a happy person, but I'd be a lot happier if people selling me things stopped trying to make me happy all the time. Buying something or using a service is often like being the only sad person at a slightly hysterical party, where everyone is having a WONDERFUL TIME, and won't stop talking in case you burst into tears and wreck everything.

This leads to the activity of creating words which make it sound like something wonderfully positive is happening, especially when it isn't. The most obnoxious example must be the spread of the term 'friendly fire', meaning being shot at by your own side in war: it sounds so terrific that it is being picked up as a metaphor in other sectors, where it also sounds militaristic, and so perfectly thrilling. There were five times as many 'friendly fire' incidents in reporting from the financial sector in 2011 as there were in 2009. I don't think they were actually shooting each other – but I've seen quite a few traders, and not much would surprise me about them.

The power of positive thinking

Why can't I write something happy and positive for a change? Who wouldn't want to read a book called 'Jargon for Fun and Pleasure', or 'Ideating Optimal Waffle: the Seven Secrets of Leading Through Confusion'?

I may mock, but those who want more happiness in their news might be getting your wish. The graph shown in Figure 4.2 is an index of how often the words 'positives' and 'negatives' show up in Factiva's global major news stories database. I've taken 2002 as the base

Figure 4.2 Index of 'positives' over 'negatives' in major news stories (2002 = 1)

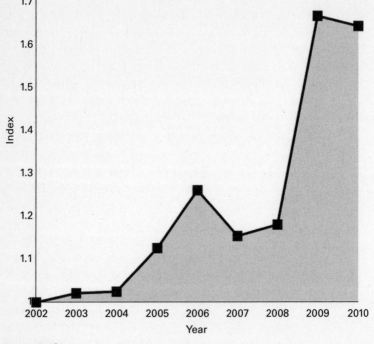

Source: Factiva

because, in 2002, there were about the same number of positives and negatives in the press.

As you can see, the graph doesn't change much until the end of 2008. Then it whizzes up. The number of stories mentioning negatives hasn't changed very much, but there are hundreds more stories mentioning positivity. We're obviously learning to look on the bright side (Figure 4.3).

I excluded sports stories from this on purpose, because I had chosen the jargon noun 'positives' (the thing that footballers 'take') rather than the more common adjective 'positive'. There are few setbacks so appalling, no disappointments too depressing that a news story can't quote someone taking positives from them.

Figure 4.3   Index of 'positives' over 'positive' in major news stories (2002 = 1)

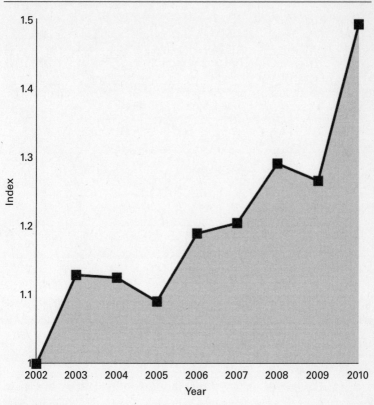

Source: Factiva

The news business is changing: it is less about what's happening, and more about how people feel about what just happened. These reactions may not be informed or relevant, but they're certainly easier to report quickly. It is news for the Facebook generation, because we can all get involved. Not only have we taken the positives, we're evidently not ready to give them back.

I can take the despair. It's the hope I can't stand[3]

There's good news and there's bad news, but there's more good news. I'm not just trying to make you feel better, there really is. I divided the number of stories mentioning 'good news' by those

Figure 4.4   Good news–bad news: back to business as usual

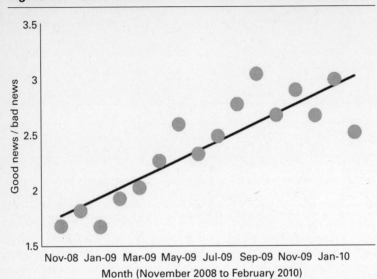

mentioning 'bad news', and there's a steady increase in good news stories since the 2008 crash (Figure 4.4).

We certainly have pluck. On this sophisticated measure, levels of non-specific hope are even higher than at the height of the boom (Figure 4.5).

It's also worth pointing out that the long-term good news ratio in the newspapers is consistently above where it was 20 years ago. And in those days newspapers were in black and white and you had to pay to read about misery rather than just ignoring it on the internet. Terrible days. Still, they didn't have Richard Littlejohn then, so not everything's changed for the better.

The press might be at a historical hope high because of the dead cat bounce theory (even a dead cat will bounce if it falls far enough: try it). In this case there is so much real-life bad news that papers have just looked harder for something chipper to write about.

Exhibit A: 'Bosses of the region's two airports say they are seeing the green shoots of recovery', said a hope-filled article in the *Newcastle Journal*, which, as far as I could see, contained almost no evidence of any green shoots at all. The article is about how the managers of local airports were hoping things would improve after average passenger numbers in the UK fell 7.4 per cent between 2009

Figure 4.5   The good news–bad news ratio in the boom

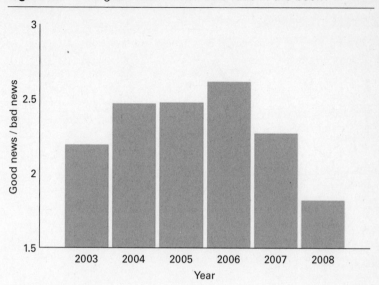

and 2010. At Newcastle Airport the drop was 9 per cent, and at Durham Tees Valley 56 per cent. If you exclude the better-performing airports, the article points out, Newcastle declined less than the average.

The technique of saying 'if we exclude all the good ones, then it's above average' is one of the most desperate, and statistically illiterate, ways to create good news. If you exclude enough of the better-performing airports, even Durham Tees performed better than the average (except that the average would have moved). That's the whole point of an average: there's as much below it as above it.

But if you're the boss you have to tell the local press that stuff is going to get better, honest. It's your job. I note that it is a journalist's job to point out when you're talking c**p (a 56 per cent decline in business is a clue in this case). But, sometimes, we all need a hug.

So it is with the 'green shoots' mentioned above, now used not as economic analysis, but as a signal of faint and desperate hope that we won't have to cook our pets for dinner or traffic the kids yet. As soon as the recession of 2008 hit, we started to look for green shoots. Business Minister Baroness Vadera in January 2009 and Solicitor

Figure 4.6   The Green Shoots Index is not peaking right now

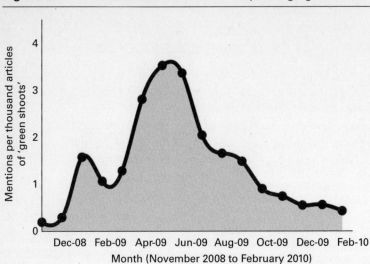

General Vera Baird in March 2009 both claimed in interviews to have spotted these shoots, which no one believed. They must have had a big magnifying glass in the UK Treasury, because gross domestic product (GDP) fell 2.64 per cent in the quarter beginning in January 2009, and 0.63 per cent the next quarter.

If you want an example of how meaningless and transient news-based optimism can be, there was a gigantic peak in UK green shoots stories in the summer of 2009, when the UK economy had no green shoots worth mentioning at all (Figure 4.6). The peak stories were mostly, in the ones I read, estate agents saying they were a bit busier.

Estate agents are the exemplars of gritted-teeth optimism. When my last landlord was selling the flat I was renting, the estate agent kept disturbing my wife and me by bringing round people to view the flat. Despite the fact that there was no benefit whatsoever to me, he couldn't help trying to sell me the benefits. It would, he told me, be a great opportunity to get that day's visit out of the way – even though there wasn't going to be a visit until he called.

But even estate agents, fanatically committed to getting to Yes!, can't keep it up forever. Note how quickly the talk of green shoots died away. You can talk unjustified happy talk all you want – but sooner or later, the truth will make a liar out of you.

Hope is a powerful drug – but it wears off quickly. Dead cats bounce; just not very high.

Don't give me problems, rename them

The most common happy word is, as you have no doubt experienced, 'solution'. There's a pervasive trend to use the word 'solution' as a way to describe the thing that a company does. *Private Eye* magazine used to run a series on it, where readers sent in baffling descriptions of ordinary jobs as impressive 'solutions'. For example:

Compost Solutions (compost)

Archaeological Solutions (the Hertfordshire Archaeological Trust)

Lingerie Solutions (lingerie)

And so on, ad infinitum. Satirist Craig Brown picked his favourite: 'Mushy Pea Fritters: the frozen versatile meal solution.'

The antitalknormalist who came up with this innovation chose 'solutions' because it's a happy word that doesn't either explain what you're doing (too many awkward questions), or tie you to any particular course of action.

I treasure an audacious and delightful innovation in the use of the S-word from the early 2000s. Hewlett-Packard's support team sent it to me when I had a problem with a printer driver (truly, I am living the dream) and I was getting a little testy in e-mails to them, because they weren't fixing it for me.

I'm accustomed to getting cut-and-paste expressions of remorse when the cable TV man doesn't bother to show up on my day off, and automated voices telling me that they are sorry, and my call is important. These are obvious and rather pathetic lies, but there's something about the obvious lack of commitment that means you shrug and move on. HP wasn't having any of that, as its e-mail shows: it decided to innovate a completely new meaning.

It shows a technical support operation that so wants to bring me good news, and so can't, that it has adopted plan B: simply redefining the word 'problem' as 'solution' and e-mailing my problem back to me to see if I'd notice. Figure 4.7 shows what it said.

Why stop at printer drivers? Innovation like this could, overnight, solve much bigger problems simply by redefining them in a more glass-half-full way. Let us be bold and agitate for Hewlett-Packard's technical support department to be given control of the biggest

Figure 4.7   Redefining the word 'problem' as 'solution'

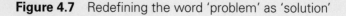

To: tim@talknormal.co.uk
Subject: Solution

Hello,

I am Sorry for the confusion about
what the term "Solution" actually
means. I think an explanation of what
"Solution" means may help.

A "Solution" is an identified,
confirmed problem. A fix for a
particular Solution will be
developed, and the fix itself made
available, at some point after a
Solution has been approved.

In this case, Solution 133893 will
probably require a change to the
program and a new "EXE" file created.
There is no fix available yet for
Solution 133893. I do not know when a
fix will be available, but it may
take some time.

I hope this helps explain why there
is no file attached to this Solution.

problem (soon to be solution) of all: world peace. It would take but a
few minutes to draft an e-mail declaring that world peace has been
achieved, with a proviso that the actual absence of 'war' might take
some time.

Of course, in the field of world peace, this would be ridiculous. It's
about as likely as the president of the United States being given the
Nobel Peace Prize, not because he had directly caused any peace so
far, but because he'd identified and confirmed the current lack of
peace, and promised to let us all know when a fix is available.

Figure 4.8 Transparency is not always an advantage.

Picture: Neil Hoggarth

On the plus side: I remember that HP did eventually e-mail me a printer driver that worked. So it stands to reason we should be optimistic about what we will soon be calling 'peace solutions'.

Seeing right through it

If you want to sound honest, it's popular to describe your organ-isation as accountable, ethical, or having integrity right now. These attributes are all twice as common in press releases as they were in 2002.

But if you're looking for the really hot happy word at the moment to show you're not a bunch of liars or crooks, then there really isn't anything to compare with saying that you provide, support or exhibit transparency (Figure 4.8) – a term which was almost unused 10 years ago. In Factiva's press release archive for 2009, one out of every 44

Figure 4.9   Transparency: vague, yet popular

press releases was claiming some sort of transparency. That's almost twice as many mentions as goody-goody integrity, and four times as many as dull old accountability. Last year a claim of some type of transparency was six times as frequent as it was in 2002, when Enron and Worldcom were on our minds (Figure 4.9).

Which industry claims the most transparency? First I looked in the obvious place: the glass manufacturing industry. Its press releases rarely claim transparency (Figure 4.10).

Banking was barely above average. Perhaps the score is dragged down because when the board admits it didn't even understand the risks the banks faced in 2007 and 2008 (Citigroup, for example), it's hard for them to claim too much transparency a year or two later. Software press releases, where so many vague buzzwords are popularised, scored higher (Figure 4.11).

Political press releases optimistically mention transparency far more than the average, which is wonderful. I should note that I originally performed this research in the week that an ex-minister was secretly filmed telling fake lobbyists he was a 'cab for hire' to peddle behind-the-scenes influence for £5,000 a day on behalf of business clients who wanted to make sure regulation and policy favoured them. So take it with a pinch of salt (Figure 4.12).

Figure 4.10 The glass manufacturing industry: claims of transparency in 2009

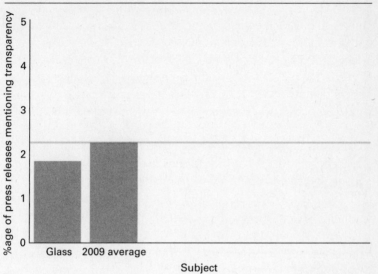

Figure 4.11 Software press releases: claims of transparency in 2009

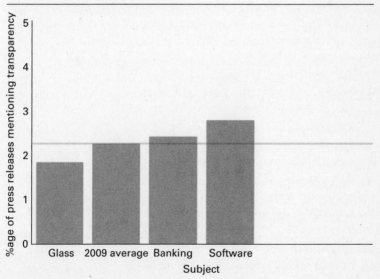

Figure 4.12   Political press releases:
claims of transparency in 2009

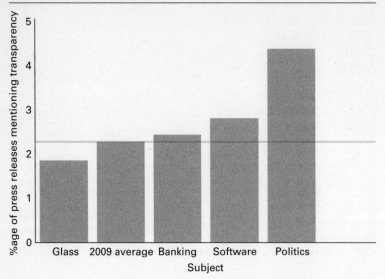

But nothing can compare, in its determination to talk about transparency, with our winning category. It was obviously a great relief to
find that, when I crunched the numbers the week after Ernst & Young
was forced to deny accusations of malpractice, negligence and
failure to exercise professional care in its audit of Lehman Brothers,
accountancy press releases were the biggest users of transparency
that I could find in 2009 – by a factor of five (Figure 4.13).

Though, perhaps, it's less reassuring to find out that E&Y alone
issued 49 press releases that mention the happy T-word since the
beginning of 2006.

Provided you are not a glass manufacturer, your actual level of
transparency is impossible to measure. It is one of those aspirational
words that anyone can claim for free. Unless, like Ernst & Young, you
are accused of helping to hide $50bn of debt for a client by the US
bankruptcy courts (for example), a claim that you exhibit accountability/
integrity/transparency will go untested.

Transparency, as the least testable of the three, is also the most
useful in this regard.

So good news for those of you who work for unaccountable,
integrity-lite companies, if indeed such frightful companies exist: if
you want to claim some fake transparency in a press release, nobody

Figure 4.13 Accountancy press releases: claims of transparency in 2009

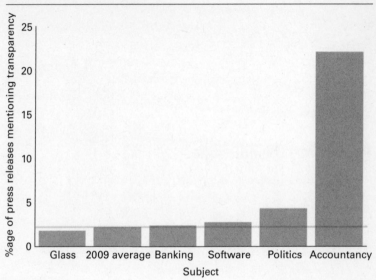

will find you out. After all, by definition, a lack of transparency is pretty hard to spot.

Shiny new things

It's easier to make us happy by showing us new stuff: on Tuesday, your smartphone is useful and practical and has simplified your life enormously. On Wednesday, the new version is launched, which is 3mm thinner and has a brighter screen. By Thursday, you're telling people that your old phone is a piece of junk, it doesn't work properly, and as soon as you can you're getting an upgrade: even though it's only a year since you queued for hours to get the one you have now, it cost you £500, and there's nothing wrong with it.

The press encourages you. New things are something fresh to write about, and so it's natural to overstate the difference that this tiny bit of innovation will do – it makes the writer, and the publication, seem relevant.

Social media's echo chamber also helps, for the same reason – but the people who are most excited are the most likely to post and tweet, creating a cacophony of excitement, like a children's party after the sugary foods come out. Then, as fanboi bloggers bounce off the roof, the press (who the older Talknormalist still can't help feeling would be the responsible adults in the room) use this as a cue to increase their excitement. Imagine your five-year-old's party if the parents, instead of sheltering wearily in the kitchen with a can of lager, started running around with the kids, screaming incoherently.

This is the atmosphere in which innovation is sold to us. So it's not surprising that so few of the companies that do the innovating are able to Talk Normal about it.

Redefining the envelope

If you are about to launch a product, an important boast is that you have 'redefined' something. There's a lot more redefinition going on these days (Figure 4.14).

In 2009 there were about two and a quarter times as many re-definitions in the PR Newswire press release database, which is the base for this graph, as there were in 2002. It's no longer enough just to be something: you also have to pretend that you've also made it impossible for anything else to be it either. In the hope that you don't

Figure 4.14 Press release 'redefinition' frequency, 2002 to 2009

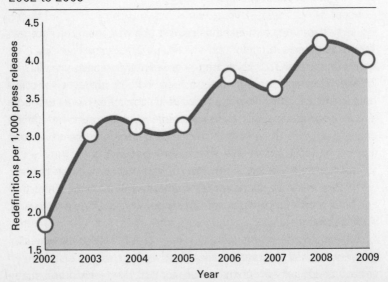

take the advice at face value, here are the things to remember if you are going to sell me a redefinition.

Add extra qualifying words that fulfil no purpose whatsoever. This, I believe, is what people call adding value. If you're going to go to the trouble of redefining a category, why not 'radically' or 'fundamentally' redefine it, to give yourself an advantage over the ordinary redefiners? I'm assuming that whoever writes your press release charges extra for this, so wait until they go home and sneak it in.

Sometimes there isn't even time to define the thing before it is redefined. Innovation moves so fast these days. For example, the press release that I received announcing that Sikorsky is claiming to 'Redefine the Future of Vertical Flight'.

This is a good example of what it takes to make your redefinition minimally credible. We're talking about 'credibility' in the sense that 'people won't spontaneously burst out laughing', so it's a low bar, but this is the world you made for yourself. So define the thing to be redefined as narrowly as possible, while still keeping people interested. If you go big, and claim to have 'redefined food', success may prove elusive. On the other hand, you have a shot if you are claiming to have 'redefined the budget chicken-based instant noodle sector'.

It's an obscure point of logic, but if we allow the definition of a category to change each time a new example of something that fits into that category comes along, then we also redefine the concept of 'definition'. What seems like nothing more than a bad press release may also be undermining analytic philosophy product by tedious product.

Meanwhile at The North Face, Chris Fanning, executive director of The Outdoor Foundation, is claiming that its 'online resource' (a website) means that 'young leaders from across the country will be empowered to reclaim, redefine and rediscover the outdoors'.[4] I quite like the outdoors and the online resource is admirable, but I'd have to quibble with the extent of the redefinition. Tell me if I'm wrong, but surely the only way for me to 'redefine' the outdoors is to move my door? Even that seems like pretty small beer.

I'm sure this online resource will empower young leaders to learn a lot about the outdoors – with the limitation that they'll unfortunately be indoors while they're doing it – but I fret that many will be disappointed when they realise they can't actually 'redefine' it yet. The rest of us can take comfort from the fact that the outdoors will still be out there, as unredefined as it was before overwrought copywriting was invented.

A state of permanent revolution

If you're going to redefine something, then you could argue that your widget is 'revolutionary'. Well, if you're an overexcited moron, you could.

Even if you don't, there are many people so stimulated by technology that they would call a new plug adapter 'revolutionary'.[5]

The best example from recent times of this has been the launch of the Apple iPad. It may turn out to be an important piece of computer hardware, but there were no shortage of news outlets that were willing to pronounce it 'revolutionary' before they even knew what it looked like. In fact, the articles declared a revolution before the thing that was causing the revolution even had a name.[6]

When faced with the *Guardian* article for the launch, which asked some half-famous people which way up they held their iPad (India Knight, columnist: 'Depends on the app, but mostly horizontally'), we could conclude that this was mainly a revolution in meaningless gibberish.

Would the human race ever be the same ever again, except for the 10 million people in the UK who have never used the internet, the one-third of Europeans who haven't either, or the 4 billion people in the world who've never even used a phone (let alone used one to download an app to tell them where the nearest sushi bar is)?

In the developed world, we organise our revolutions around the availability of consumer electronics these days, so I thought I'd look into how good Apple and Microsoft, the chino-wearing Bolsheviks of this revolutionary era, have been at getting us to mount the barricades for their respective revolutions.

The first chart (Figure 4.15) shows how well, over the past 10 years, the companies have been doing at converting claims that they are revolutionary into news stories that agree with the premise. I restricted this to technology news in newspapers. The line zigs about a bit, but as you can see Microsoft wasn't making much headway until Windows 7 got journalists a bit excited – although the line shoots up mostly because there were far fewer Microsoft press releases claiming a revolution than there were in 2008 (when it did

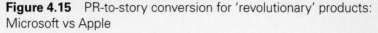

Figure 4.15   PR-to-story conversion for 'revolutionary' products: Microsoft vs Apple

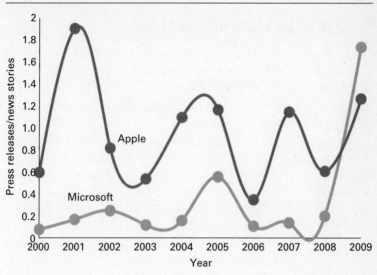

nothing particularly revolutionary at all, but was twice as likely to claim that it did).

The second chart (Figure 4.16) takes claims for revolution in any year and subtracts Microsoft's coverage from Apple's. If the dot is in the top half of the graph, Apple is winning. In the bottom half, it's Microsoft. It shows that while journalists are more comfortable saying that Apple was starting a revolution (purple line: top half for the whole decade), Apple's PR too (orange line) is becoming increasingly comfortable with this particular example of meaningless hyperbole. At the beginning of the decade Apple almost never claimed to be revolutionary. Now, perhaps encouraged by the willingness of journalists to pass on the message through oracles such as India Knight, it is three times as likely as Microsoft to claim its products are revolutionary.

I'm sure that in the old days we would have waited until we had actually seen the product before we decided that something was going to cause a revolution. The Segway, of course, was an exception.

In the interests of full disclosure, I'm typing this on my iMac while syncing iTunes with my iPhone. But I haven't got an iPad, so I can't tell you which way up I hold it: please try to soldier on.

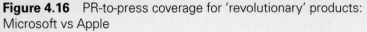

Figure 4.16   PR-to-press coverage for 'revolutionary' products: Microsoft vs Apple

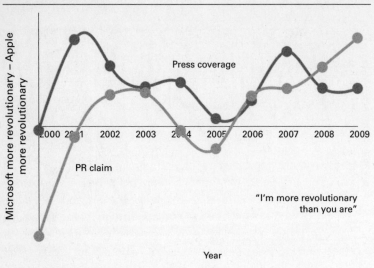

The game-changing game has changed for game-changers

The revolution is sometimes delayed: in January 2010, soon after Apple launched the iPad, Google launched a phone. But not just any old phone: Google launched a 'game-changing' phone called the Nexus One.

Never heard of it? That's because it didn't change any games. It wasn't even quite clear what game the Nexus One was playing. By the end of the summer the phone had been so unsuccessful that Google had withdrawn it from sale.

I'm not sure that anyone has explained to me the specific game that mobile phone companies are playing (though if my recent experience with Orange Mobile Broadband is any guide, one version of the rules is called Shaft The Customer), but 147 articles in the telecommunications press around the launch described Google as changing an unspecified game.

This is, lest we forget, after Apple has already changed a similar game. The 249 articles which describe Apple in the same way peaked in 2007, so we must assume in this case that Google is re-re-changing

Figure 4.17   Game-changingness: telecoms press

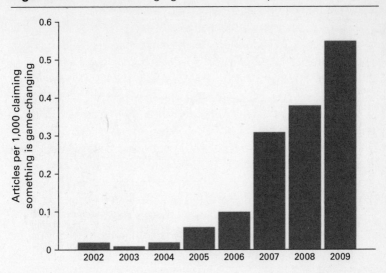

the game that Apple re-changed after Nokia changed it after someone else invented it.

When we look at telecommunications in general, few games have been left unchanged in the past two or three years. Around 2002 or 2003 it was very unusual to find anything in the telecommunications press that claimed to change any game at all. We had 30 times as many game-changers in 2009, compared to what we would have expected had game-changingness remained at 2002 levels (Figure 4.17).

It isn't just telecommunications in which companies are claiming to have altered the game as soon as the previous permutation of the earlier mutation of the last modification has taken effect. Figure 4.18 shows the trend in the business press, where we find companies that change games about half as frequently, but with a similar upward trend. In 2009 we got only about 20 times as much game-changingness as we would have expected, taking 2002 as our base.

Part of this is journalistic over-stimulation: the increasing resemblance of business reporting to a Mexican soap opera. So given that some reporters are willing to write up the opening of a jar of pickle as potentially game-changing, marketers are helping by using the term

Figure 4.18 Game-changingness: business press

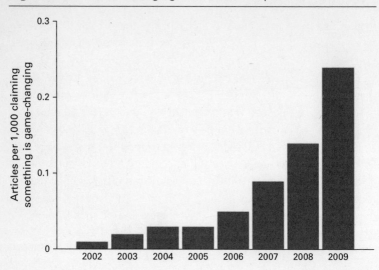

game-changing to play the most important media game of all: the game of Pump Up What Your Employer Does To Make It Sound More Important Than Selling A Product. You might say that their use of game-changing has, in itself, been game-changing. If you wanted me to slap you, that is.

The buzzword wars

Encouraging us to buy things means giving us reasons to buy: if you are launching a mobile phone, for example, then there's at least something you can hold up that didn't exist yesterday. We can recognise this as change.

Now imagine you're marketing something that people don't seem to want, can't afford, and isn't any different to what it was last year. In this circumstance, you can't call it game-changing or revolutionary. The trick is to make up a silly name for it. Some of our finest minds are involved in this, and plenty of the dull ones too.

All together now

In the history of mergers and acquisitions, there's one that stands head and shoulders above the rest as a disaster: AOL and Time Warner.

I did some research into the merger for my previous book[7] and one thing stands out: the number of reporters who faithfully wrote down that the two businesses would capitalise on their 'synergies', without really asking what those synergies might actually, you know, be.

Synergy is a happy weasel word. It sounds like something marvellous is going to happen and, when it does, there is much money to be made – for shareholders, at least. What most people see are redundancies (there's no synergy without redundancy), and selling the buildings that they worked in. It is also a vague placeholder for 'we want some of their stuff to make our stuff work better'.

In the first case, using it avoids awkward words like redundancy that make people glum, and in the second, it avoids actually telling us what they are going to do.

So it's a great way to sell a merger. There are good reasons for vagueness: until the deal's done, synergy is a best-guess kind of prediction. The buyer doesn't know where the bodies are buried.

I went back to the Factiva database to see whether there are more businesses claiming synergy these days, and there are, big time. I searched in the European and North American business press, and compared the number of articles mentioning mergers with the number mentioning mergers and synergies too. Merger and acquisition (M&A) volumes may have gone off a cliff during 2008–10, but the synergy bubble never bursts. Mentions of synergy are 402 per cent up in the last 30 years, and the rise has been wonderfully consistent (Figure 4.19).

In just over 30 years it has become five times as likely that a business will describe a merger as providing synergies (or, at least, that this lazy rebranding will be reported in the press).

It might just be that synergy has become a vogue word. But I think it's also due to positive word bias, which is far more of a problem.

To explain: every M&A deal has some rationale beyond a pooling of capital and saving on letterheads. The benefits can be difficult to explain, easy to question, or impossible to measure accurately: three reasons not to go into too much detail if you want to push it through quickly – especially if you're directly or indirectly incentivised to make

Figure 4.19 The percentage of articles mentioning mergers vs the number mentioning both mergers and synergies, January 1979 to the present

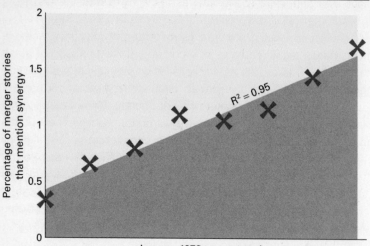

the merger work. If you want to create momentum in the media or among shareholders and employees (and in your own mind) it helps to give the benefits a positive-sounding, catchy, go-for-it name.

This wouldn't matter so much if it wasn't for the problem that companies tend to overpay for their acquisitions. One reason they overpay is that they start to believe the over-optimistic assumptions that they peddled to create the deal. They believe their own happy words.

That name is synergy: code for the things we don't really want to talk about right now. It won't make your merger work any better, but it might make more people believe that it will.

And remember: if you're working for the bank that puts it together – or any other of the support organisations that prop up the deal – and so your reward comes more from the deal than the messy aftermath: it pays to talk about synergy.

Selling empowerment by the pound

If you're sad because you lack power, don't worry. There are a lot of people who can sell you something for that.

This isn't really the point of a word that once described how you give victims of discrimination or poverty the ability to change their lives. It's 'empowerment' in the sense that if you buy a pair of jeans from me, I empower you to wear some new trousers.

Or, rather: 'Possession of the Talk Normal LegRight Solution (TM) empowers the global community of potential denim-wearers to actualise our jeans dreams!'

Whether it's from the ambitiously named Empower MediaMarketing ('Understanding is the bottom line'), which among other recent empowerments organised a Discovery Channel Shark Week promotion for Long John Silver Fish Tacos, or the Ladies' Professional Golf Association ('to inspire, empower, educate and entertain by showcasing the best golf professionals in the world'), or even the Center for Applied Identity Management Research's ongoing efforts 'to empower and engage with clients in combating identity theft crimes and mitigating fraud', there's a lot of empowerment available – if you can pay for it.

Empowerment had an ethical and political meaning, which doesn't have much relevance to tacos or golf. Instead, the releases that mention empowerment on the press release collection at PR Newswire confirm that empowerment usually involves a commercial transaction.

It's a happy word that seems like it was always here, but it wasn't. Empowerment went almost unmentioned until 1980, then quickly became pervasive (Figure 4.20).

Maybe it's no longer enough to sell us a product, we have to buy a better life too.

Marketers have hijacked the idea of empowerment to do this, because it's a no-risk proposition. 'We don't make promises,' these empowerers tell us, 'we just sell you something to help you change yourself.'

They don't make you happy; but they are willing, for a fee, to claim they empower you to achieve happiness. It's not their fault if you're too stupid, ugly, poor (or powerless) to make the best of it.

Commercial empowerment: if it works they take the credit. If it doesn't, that's your problem.

Should have stayed in bed

How are buzzwords made? Usually, by people whose job it is to invent or popularise them. I offer in evidence the failed attempt by

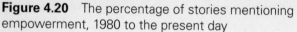

Figure 4.20 The percentage of stories mentioning empowerment, 1980 to the present day

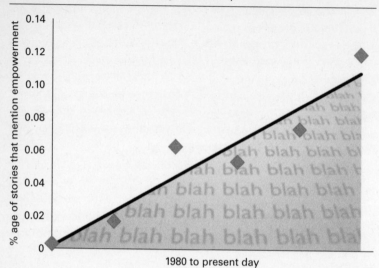

holiday operator Thomson to popularise the phrase 'awaycation' to describe a holiday overseas. We need some good news, so when Thomson tried this sad little stunt in April 2010, we can be encouraged that even journalists groaned and pretended it wasn't happening. I could find only four publications that wrote about it – and one of them only printed the word to make fun of it. Talknormalists, take heart.

The awaycation is the latest shot in marketing's tedious Buzzword Wars. Imagine, if you will, a group of dedicated marketers and PR people in early 2008, huddled in a meeting room, desperately trying to make the prospect of a week in Scarborough seem attractive to people who would prefer to take their leisure in Ibiza or Florida.

There's a reason why we choose not to go on holiday to the same places that our parents visited. It's broadly speaking because, compared to most popular destinations in the world, a British holiday is what travel experts call 'a bit c**p'.

But call your holiday a 'staycation' and you're not just eating overpriced jumbo haddock and chips while watching the drizzle, you're part of a global economic trend. Also, it gives the travel section something to write about, because they did the South of France last month and the budget's shot and they couldn't cadge a free flight to write about Dubrovnik.

The tedious buzzword magic worked for the staycation marketers – seven uses of the word before January 2008, more than 4,000 in the two years afterwards – so in 2010 Thomson, which owns 77 planes and even bought a Boeing 787, needed to work the same magic. Not least because staycations, though useful for people without much money who have umbrellas and warm clothes, are disastrous for travel firms who want you to fly to Cancun on their plane for two weeks all-in at their hotel.

The brief (I'm guessing):

1 It must sound like 'staycation'.

2 Except that it has to involve getting on an aeroplane.

Hence, the 'awaycation'. That's why they are earning the big bucks, and you're reading a sarcastic book. Take the rest of the day off, holiday company marketers, your work here is done.

This tedious rebirthing isn't new, because there are so many reasons beyond inspiration-free desperation for marketers to do it. It might just be the self-importance that turns a personnel department into human resources. It might be a way to do an about-turn without making it look like you were wrong, which turns outsourcing into insourcing, rightsourcing or even upsourcing (it exists, but I can't really describe it in a way that makes sense).

Or, sadly, it might be our need to see every event in our lives as a jolly project with a special name and a happy ending. Losing your job has always been a pain for you and an opportunity for buzzword manufacturers. In vogue at the moment: you're not being forced in middle age to take a job for which you don't have the skills or experience you need, that's depressing and sad and might have an unhappy ending. No, you are 're-careering', which sounds much better, and far more likely to succeed.

If you have expertise in inventing pointless words for marketing purposes but currently find yourself unavoidably re-careering, perhaps a job in an expanded Ministry of Euphemisms for Bad Things is on the cards. On the evidence of the UK general election of 2010 trying to pretend that it's OK really is one part of the public sector that has continued to expand in the recession. If we're going to fight the Buzzword Wars, our troops need to have the right euphemisms. Sorry, I meant they need to be optimally resourced with appropriately context-sensitive descriptors.

These meaningless government phrases don't invent themselves, you know: someone has to organise the use of 'negative growth' for a business slump, and 'revenue enhancement' for more tax.

Some of the battles of the buzzword wars have been so comprehensively lost, we forget they ever needed to be fought. We no longer raise an eyebrow when a retreat is called a 'Strategic withdrawal', and the 'Ministry of Defence' makes the announcement. Maybe it helps us sleep at night.

But it isn't inevitable that Talknormalism will lose the Buzzword Wars. When the US Constitution called slavery 'Involuntary servitude', it didn't fool anyone. Obviously it took almost 200 years to sort that one out, but it's a bigger problem than where you're going on holiday this year.

A quick search shows that even the mildly silly 're-careering' had a better run in the press than 'awaycation' has, so far at least. I find this encouraging: we have discovered that it is possible to come up with a marketing buzzword that's so obviously rubbish that everyone simply ignores it, like a bad smell.

Why computer software is like a drunk Viking

Leadership manuals encourage us to speak in metaphors to inspire those around us: they explain and inspire. In my experience they more often bore and confuse, because it's hard to come up with a new metaphor when you have a job to do already, so you grab for one that someone like you said last week.

A basic, and fundamental, problem with faddy jargon phrases that you pick up this way is that sooner or later, you're going to find someone who doesn't know what on earth you're talking about. This is great if you are a youth and want to confuse people like me. It's not so good if you are a manager and succeed in confusing your staff and your bosses. It's worst of all if your job is to explain something: you don't want to explain it solely to the 'in group'.

There's a shameful pleasure that we never lose in confusing other people with a phrase. We remember the feeling of satisfaction from school: it would be strange if we suddenly abandoned it later. Last

Figure 4.21   Google labs: Books Ngram Viewer

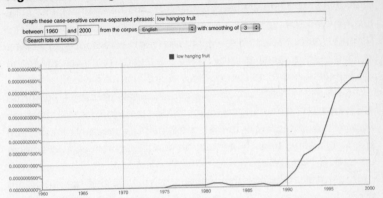

week I admit that I said something was 'copacetic', just so the other fortysomethings in the room could say: 'I haven't heard that one for ages', while anyone too young to have watched *Buffy the Vampire Slayer* looked confused. If you have the same expression, it means 'satisfactory'.[8]

Even if everyone knows what you are talking about, vogueish metaphors are often either tired or trite. At any time we pick up a set of fashionable phrases, but use them too much – and so they become far less informative than just describing the thing talknormally.

Some hang around long after we tire of them: I've never met anyone who claims they enjoy talking about low-hanging fruit, but I'm obviously hanging with the wrong homies, because it's more popular than ever (Figure 4.21).

Tired phrases gradually lose their impact (the idea of a metaphor is, ideally, to surprise you into thinking about a concept in a new way). They quickly begin to grate, too. You think you sound terrific. Other people are, at best, baffled.

Someone sent this Tweet to me, to ask for an explanation: 'It's becoming very clear that enterprise apps and databases will be the "straw that stirs the drink" in the enterprise server refresh cycle.'

That is, in the current vogue phrase, a Big Ask. I can't really explain what the point of Twitter is, let alone individual tweets. But this tweet came from an analyst, whose job is defined as explaining things, so I was interested to see if I could explain what he was explaining.

I'm delighted to hear that enterprise apps are the straw that stirs. I just don't really know what I'm hearing. I was worried that everyone else knew what being a straw that stirs a drink was and I didn't, so when I started to type the phrase into Google, I was pleased that it immediately suggested, from previous searches, 'what does the straw that stirs the drink mean?'

At the same time, I was on a conference call, and someone asked what his job in a meeting was. Someone else offered the suggestion that he was going to be the straw that stirred the drink. Forty-three years of not hearing it, then twice in a week. I needed a Google education.

The Urban Dictionary suggested that it was a term used to describe someone who is the life of the party, and suggests 'Party Viking' as an alternative – which I like much more, as 'databases will be the "Party Viking" in the enterprise server refresh cycle' suggests that some software is even now wearing a little plastic helmet with horns on it. It is stripped to the waist and barfing behind your data centre's sofa. I don't think that's what the analyst meant, but I wish it was.

The journal *Strategy and Leadership* had an article about PepsiCo management, which used the straw–drink analogy as its title. The abstract explained the process of being the straw that stirs the drink as: 'Strategic Planning is clearly a line function at PepsiCo'. Clearly this concept is not all about Viking hats.

At eLearn University I consulted 'The Defining Moment: The Straw That Stirs The Drink Of Motivational Leadership' to learn that 'There are three ways to transfer your motivation to others. Give them information, make sense...' and then I gave up before I got to 'how to tell the story of your Defining Moment', lacking as I was in motivation to finish the sentence. They tell you this at Leadership University? God knows what they teach at Leadership Remedial School. How to answer a Big Ask, probably.

And I also find that, according to *The Hidden Meaning of Birthdays* by Nancy Arnott, Geminis are this type of straw – as long as they are Geminis who were born on 20 June. Think of the Party Vikings she suggests like Errol Flynn, er, Nicole Kidman or, um, Lionel Ritchie. According to Arnott, people born on this day are inevitably straws that stir drinks, which suggests a possible management fast-tracking strategy at PepsiCo: get Ritchie in. He'll kick ass All Night Long.

But back to these 20 June Geminis: 'Expressing your passionate feelings tends to churn up strong emotions in those around you... every event at work and on the home front elicits a Richter-scale reaction from you', she says; which sounds about as unlike Kidman or Ritchie as it's possible to get, and doesn't help me discover what enterprise apps are supposed to be doing.

But what do I know? I don't even understand a phrase that can be variously used to describe acting like a Viking, the process of strategic planning at a multinational consumer packaged goods company, talking about yourself under the pretence that you're inspiring people, exuding earth-trembling passion in the style of Nicole Kidman or, to bring us back to where we started, making it obvious to people that their old computers are too slow and they need to buy new ones.

Sugar pill cynicism

We dealt earlier with the main attraction for many executives of corporate social responsibility: the fact that it might turn a profit. This interpretation of what a business is here to do is easier to argue for a bank, say, which was created to make money and doesn't have any other products, than it is for a company that sells medicine.

I'm talking about a problem that's right at the heart of Talknormalism's objection to the way our language has been stolen from us by people who want to sell us stuff. I'm talking about the selling of homeopathy.

In the UK there's the 10:23 Campaign: consumers go to a pharmacy, buy homeopathic products, and overdose on them.

A quick backgrounder: homeopathy, ridiculed by journalists when it was invented in the 19th century,[9] was based on the idea that you take a substance that caused your problem, and then dilute it in a solution until it is no longer dangerous. Then dilute it some more. Then, on the assumption that the effect is stronger the more it is diluted, dilute it more than that.

A shop-bought homeopathic remedy will, on average, not have a single molecule of the active ingredient in it. It may produce a placebo effect, which is a good thing – and you could argue that the rubbish that's talked about homeopathy is useful, if it produces this effect. On the other hand, this is serious: homeopathic clinics in Africa, the World Health Organisation warns, recommend the treatments for HIV, TB and malaria instead of conventional drugs.

If you can't believe that homeopathy is silly you're unlikely to be convinced by me.

In the developed world, where there are fewer people going to the pharmacy to get something for TB or malaria, we have the luxury to consider our drug regimen a lifestyle choice. So our largest high-street chemist, Boots, makes a different argument: if the pills don't actively harm people, and customers like to buy them, why shouldn't Boots sell them?

This, ultimately, is why Talking Normal is important.

Boots has a privileged position in the UK which allows it to make surplus profits as long as it acts ethically. To explain: when I was researching *Scoring Points*,[10] my book about what Tesco did with its Clubcard data, I heard how Tesco discovered that its young female customers often stopped buying products from the pharmacy aisle for no obvious reason. Tesco did some more research, and discovered that they were going to Boots instead. What suddenly sent them to Boots? They were pregnant, and more concerned about their health. Even though Boots was, on average, 20 per cent more expensive, they valued it as one of the few retailers that they trusted to do more than just sell them stuff.

Which is why it's ethically not good enough for Boots to admit to the parliamentary Science and Technology Committee in November 2009 that there is no evidence that homeopathic remedies are effective, but continue to profit from them ('I have no evidence to suggest they are efficacious. It's about consumer choice and a large number of our customers think they work' is the quote from Paul Bennett, professional standards director). It's an example of how customer service is mutating from 'we're here to help because sound advice is more important than short-term financial gain for you and us' (the reason why the mums-to-be swapped from Tesco to Boots, or what banks used to do) to 'If you're paying, then we'll give it to you, and dress it up as something that's positive from your point of view'.

In the first case, the sort of brand trust that Boots enjoys has a meaning, and can conceivably justify charging higher prices than a supermarket. In the second, the Boots brand is just a label to help separate you from your disposable income.

Boots certainly isn't the only company that's going down this path, and maybe commercial homeopathy is small beer in the face of the Great Branding Cynicism of the early years of the 21st century. When it comes to cynical marketing, it's not as if Big Pharma's got clean hands. This is, after all, an industry that has invested resources in defining conditions such as 'female sexual dysfunction' and 'night eating syndrome', in order to create a market for the pills that 'cure' it.[11]

Homeopaths seem, in my experience of them, to be pleasant people who believe in what they are doing. Good for them. Boots, on the other hand, doesn't seem to believe in homeopathy as anything more than a source of revenue from gullible people – and for that it deserves any bad publicity it receives.

Talknormalise me

The trouble with marketing: it's not in our control, unless you work in marketing. It's also an essential part of the way businesses are made. I'm not advocating that companies just put all their stuff out and wait for people to walk past by chance, like a global yard sale. Though if CEOs were forced to sit in a deckchair, watching people making fun of their ratty stuff, it might make them a little more tolerable in their pumped-up keynote speeches.

I believe that some companies are ruining it for the rest of us. Wrap tape over their mouths, and the world would be a more Talknormal place.

A hot air blower

There's a lot of technology marketing. Part of this is because of the 'fast start' principle: if you want to innovate, and you are associated with an idea – even if seven other companies turn up with it at around the same time – you get to be a market leader, and make all the money. The dot-commers tested this to destruction by often omitting to provide the product afterwards, but they held some amazing parties, so I'm told. Hey, if you can remember the dot-com revolution, it means you weren't there.

Much technology marketing is also innovative, and widely copied. They showed fusty old brands how to segment their customers effectively, so we don't get too much communication that isn't relevant. They were the first to do commonplace things, such as the way Amazon automatically recommends what other people like you bought.

Figure 4.22   Comparing frequency of jargon phrases in US press releases, tech-specific vs general population, 2009

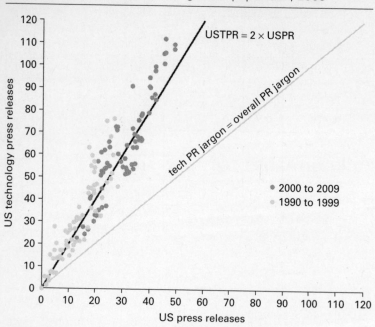

Source: Factiva

They also create a lot of hot air. A bit more analysis on the words used in the previous section: plot the relative frequency of jargon in technology PR against the frequency in US-based PR as a whole, and you get Figure 4.22.

Over a period of 20 years, technology PR has contained twice as much jargon as the norm. I'm using 'norm' to mean 'not normal, but what people like them are doing'. It's like if there was an Amazon for jargon, and when the tech-marketing people were putting together the press release, it came up with the message 'People that use the gobbledy-gook you use also like to use the following meaningless phrases...'

The evidence from the same test suggests further that a few people ruin it for the rest of us. This table of jargon that I compiled at the same time demonstrates it (Figure 4.23).

What can it mean? Read across the row. There's a 3.7 per cent chance that a press release will use robust. But, if it also describes something as next generation, it is three times as likely (10 per cent)

Figure 4.23 The more jargon you use,
the more you're likely to use

	All data	NG+	NG+F+	NG+F+R+	NG+F+R +WC+	NG+F+R +WC+S+	NG+F+R +WC+S +ETU+
Next generation	4.2						
Flexible	3.7	11.4					
Robust	3.7	10.3	17.0				
World Class	3.1	7.2	9.1	10.0			
Scalable	2.1	8.9	24.3	30.8	44.2		
Easy to use	2.2	4.8	8.3	12.4	20.9	26.3	
Cutting edge	2.1	6.4	7.3	11.4	11.6	15.8	–

it will chuck in robust as well. And if it describes something as next generation and flexible, now there's a 17 per cent chance you will find robust in there as well.

In short, the more jargon you use, the more you're likely to use.

We get to the silly situation where, having described the product or service – or, I'm willing to wager, the solution – as next generation, flexible, robust, world class and scalable, more than a quarter of press releases chuck in 'easy to use' as well.

I have three explanations why the press releases might need to call on 'easy to use' in this situation:

1 It's really important for sales: the company thinks that something which is next generation, flexible, robust, world class and scalable might sell badly because we worry that we won't find the on switch.

2 Ease of use is not an obvious feature: if you can't even write a press release that ordinary people can understand, it's unlikely we will believe you can make a product that ordinary people can use.

3 Once I watched a TV report on how they used to typeset Mao-era Chinese communist newspapers. Because the Mandarin alphabet has a basic vocabulary of more than 3,000

characters it was easier for the typesetters to keep entire ready-made Cultural Revolution jargon phrases at hand, like the one at the top of the last page, and just assemble the daily paper from the revolutionary brainwashing twaddle kit with a few names thrown in.

When we close our minds we tend to rely on empty, grandiose phrases to please authority. Of course, in the West we'd never do anything like that, because here we are free to choose which words we use. I wish more of us would take advantage of our freedom.

Notes

1   An excellent poster by Modern Toss that may offend:
    http://bit.ly/TNbuymore
2   Read it here, and relive the moment I discovered my own version of
    Tutankhamun's tomb: http://bit.ly/TNworstevah
3   John Cleese
4   http://prn.to/redefiner
5   Like these people did: http://bit.ly/notrevolutionary
6   Like this one http://bit.ly/ipadrev1, this one
    http://bit.ly/ipadrev2, or this one http://bit.ly/ipadrev3
7   *Fit to Bust: How Great Companies Fail* (Kogan Page)
8   The Google Ngram viewer (see Appendix) shows that use of the
    word peaked between 1979 and 1981 when I was a teenager,
    dropped sharply, and has since been steadily rising.
9   Read *Extraordinary Popular Delusions* by Charles MacKay to find
    that, contrary to what we assume, the Victorians also knew quack
    medicine when they saw it.
10 *Scoring Points: How Tesco Continues to Win Customer Loyalty*
    (Kogan Page)
11 More on this at the Bad Science blog: http://badscience.net

Appendix: heroes of Talknormalism

Ten books that help

There are many books about how to make a good presentation. There are even a few that tell you how to run a conference call well. You can find them yourself. Instead I've picked out some books that you might have missed which are informative and enjoyable enough to read on the bus.

Why Truth Matters
Ophelia Benson and Jeremy Stangroom, Continuum Books (2006)

It matters, the book tells us, 'because we are the only species we know of that has the ability to find it out'. It sets out to 'fight fashionable nonsense' in a wonderful polemic which deals with the popular idea that everything is a matter of opinion. You might not care very much about postmodernism or relativism, and the arguments that the philosophers who popularised those ideas proposed. But when those arguments provide a voice for Holocaust deniers in the media or creationists in schools, there is undoubtedly a problem that needs to be solved.

Essential English for Journalists, Editors and Writers
Harold Evans, Pimlico (2000)

I mentioned this several times in the book, with good reason. It's a practical guide to how to write clearly. It was originally written for 'newsmen' at a time when there were few 'newswomen', but it has been kept up to date. It's not fusty and it doesn't try to preserve a lost language, unlike many grammar guides. It's useful for everyone who wants to improve – but be warned: you can't just buy it. You have to read it too.

Flat Earth News
Nick Davies, Chatto & Windus (2008)

'The news will never be the same again', it promises, and if you want to know why the news is the way it is, it's the best 'insider's guide'. Davies continues to work as an investigative journalist, but he picks apart the lazy, clichéd news stories that reinforce our prejudices and feed us misinformation. Talknormalism isn't simply a matter of which word goes where.

OBD: Obsessive Branding Disorder
Lucas Conley, PublicAffairs (2008)

It's a $300 billion industry, but branding is seen by outsiders simply as a choice of packaging or a new product name. It's about more than handbags, though. Conley explains how everything is consciously branded today, how the choice of words manipulates our opinions of ourselves and the world around us, and how 'a stratagem gone wrong' feeds us misinformation and bias.

Evolving English
David Crystal, The British Library (2011)

In 2011, the British Library staged an exhibition of the history of the English language. This illustrated book accompanied it, but can be read on its own. Professor Crystal is an expert on the history of the language, and the book has examples of how it has evolved. What does this have to teach us? That we shouldn't be stick-in-the-muds about new phrases or words, just because they are new. The language has been changing continuously for hundreds of years, and we're just temporary custodians of it.

Talk Normal isn't about complaining because someone moved the language when we weren't looking. It's about exposing (and eliminating) the abuse of language to manipulate or confuse us, who does it, and why powerful people benefit from it. Read this book, and you'll realise that this, too, has been going on for centuries.

Information is Beautiful
David McCandless, Collins (2010)

A beautiful and justifiably popular book: 'We need a new way to discover the beauty and the fun of information'. McCandless is a journalist who has discovered that the picture often gives us an insight in ways that words cannot. Read the book, look at the diagrams, then go to work and look at the PowerPoint slides you use.

Talk Normal is primarily about the words we choose to use, but words in their best order are still not the best way to tell some stories.

Lies, and the Lying Liars Who Tell Them
Al Franken, Plume (2004)

He's US senator Al Franken now, but when he wrote this he was mostly known as a comedian. So it's surprising that in a book about how the powerful twist words and manipulate stories in the mass media, he did his research. Or, rather, he used a group of student volunteers from Harvard University to do it. Not everyone will like his conclusions, because Franken's target is the political right wing: but you have to respect the evidence he brings forward. And the jokes are funny, too.

The Cult of the Amateur
Andrew Keen, Nicholas Brealey Publishing (2007)

Subtitled: 'How Today's Internet Is Killing Our Culture and Assaulting Our Economy', you're not going to agree with everything in Keen's critique of blog culture. It's polemic. His idea is that internet culture is destroying craft, and making matters of right and wrong into a simple clash of ideas, where the mob rules.

You don't have to like what he says, and you don't need to agree with all of it: but it's an important book in my opinion for two reasons. It was one of the first to point out that Web 2.0 and social media can be manipulated by the powerful to rewrite the truth as much as it can democratise culture to reveal it. It also gets people discussing the subject, even if they haven't read it. Especially if they haven't read it.

Beyond Words
John Humphrys, Hodder & Stoughton (2006)

Humphrys is well known as an assertive interviewer on the Radio 4 *Today* programme, which is the first stop for politicians every morning when they want to convince us that their idea is terrific. He's a long-time champion of straight talk – which must be difficult for him, seeing as he gets up so early to hear so little of it. He has written two books on the subject of language: the first, *Lost for Words*, dealt with correct grammar. This follow-up deals with how language reveals the way we live now, based on his experiences as a journalist. It also deals with how it feels to urinate while standing next to Tony Blair, which will be an insight for at least half of the population.

Office Space
Mike Judge (1999)

Is it cheating to have a film here too? For all of you who hate your jobs, the hero, Peter Gibbons, works in a dead-end job, where the only new thing to happen is the visit of the downsizing consultants, the printer never works, and next Friday is 'Hawaiian Shirt Day' at the office. When he realises he no longer feels the need to hang on to his job and stops showing up to work, his attitude only makes him more valuable to the company. As he tells his hypnotist: 'I was sitting in my cubicle today, and I realised, ever since I started working, every single day of my life has been worse than the day before it. So that means that every single day that you see me, that's on the worst day of my life.' This will tell you more about office culture, and how to survive it, than any ten books on how to be a successful manager that you can find.

Ten websites that help

Should I have called them 'online resources'? Would more of you visit them if I had? These are the problems we must wrestle with every day, provided we have enough free time. Meanwhile, I've called them websites, because that's what they are.

The Onion
http://www.theonion.com

The best spoof news site on the web, as it has been for many years. If something is bothering you about a news story, and you don't know why, look up the Onion's spoof of it and say: 'That's why it is ridiculous'.

News stories include: 'Actual Expert too Boring', and 'Manager Achieves Full Mastery Of Pointless Managerial Jargon':

During what was described to them as 'a look-forward meeting to discuss and evaluate the company's event-chain methodology,' MediaLine employees stood with mouths agape [on] Wednesday as they witnessed the very moment at which project manager James Atkins attained complete mastery over the fine art of meaningless corporate doublespeak.

Google Books Ngram viewer
http://ngrams.googlelabs.com/

If you want to do some word sleuthing, there's nothing better. Ngram searches for your word or phrase in a giant database of millions of books. There are subsets that you can search, by country, just for fiction for example. As long as your phrase occurs in 40 books, you will get a graph of how often it has occurred in history. You can rerun some of the Talk Normal experiments to search for 500 years instead of five. Or you can do your own experiment. If you do, and it's interesting, e-mail me at **tim@timphillips.co.uk**.

Unsuck It
http://unsuck-it.com/

The best of the joke jargon sites: you type in your jargon phrase, and it translates it for you – simple as that: 'metric' becomes measurement, 'on the same page' means understanding each other, and you have to look up 'open the kimono' for yourself. If the phrase doesn't exist, you can offer a definition, or it asks the 'lazyweb' for one by tweeting it.

Adventures of Action Item
http://professionalsuperhero.com/

Not so much a website as a comic strip: the story of a goal-oriented results-driven superhero who will save the city, but not until he's addressed it in a sidebar meeting, because it's not on his list of deliverables for this milestone.

TED: Ideas worth spreading
http://www.ted.com/

The annual conference is a media favourite, because here are some people they haven't heard of who are not selling anything, and who are genuinely interesting. TED, and its spin-off conferences, invites interesting experts to tell us things we haven't heard before in a way that anyone can understand. You can watch videos of the presentations, and wish you were there. A reminder that anyone can make complicated things difficult to understand. An expert makes them sound simple. Inspirational.

Indexed
http://thisisindexed.com/

Figure A.1   A diagram that makes you think
(**http://thisisindexed.com/**)

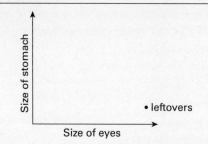

Published 'Weekday mornings as the coffee brews', Jessica Hagy's site is a collection of clever diagrams drawn on 5×7 index cards that make you think, and sometimes laugh. They remind us of a time when people drew a diagram to communicate an idea, not because they had clip art and didn't know what to do with it. Some of them are available to buy as a postcard book, and you can order your favourites as a T-shirt or a poster. Or, if you're really sensible, use the ideas to inspire your presentations.

Bad Science
http://www.badscience.net

Dr Ben Goldacre's blog is a powerful, and well-researched, antidote to pseudoscience in the media. As a 'real' doctor he knows what he is talking about, knows how to read statistics, and is prepared to track down the originators of the stories to ask them difficult questions that most journalists will never know enough about the subject to ask. This isn't just important for Talknormalists: it's a hugely important contribution to both public policy and health. Goldacre's work on subjects such as the MMR panic (and the press coverage of it), the harm done by illegal drugs, and the government's policies on health – whichever government is in power – are unlike anything else in the media. There is also a Bad Science book, which goes into more depth on some of the most important subjects his blog has investigated.

spEak You're bRanes
http://ifyoulikeitsomuchwhydontyougolivethere.com/

'A collection of ignorance, narcissism, stupidity, hypocrisy and bad grammar' is the description, and they've never been more fun. SYB takes the nuttiest quotes from online message boards – it started by exclusively concentrating on the BBC 'Have Your Say' board, but now spreads its net wide – and presents them to us so we don't have to go looking for them. I once visited the room in which the moderators for these message boards worked. All I could think was, 'if SYB reprints the stuff you let through, what on earth must you be taking out?' On balance, I'd prefer not to know.

Adbusters
http://www.adbusters.org

'We are a global network of culture jammers and creatives working to change the way information flows, the way corporations wield power, and the way meaning is produced in our society.' I don't know what a culture jammer is, but I'm in. Adbusters has some excellent spoof advertisements (and produces a calendar of them every year), runs campaigns like 'Buy Nothing Day' (no purchase necessary), and runs blogs and videos that will make you question the marketing trash that litters our culture. If they weren't so well organised and energetic, the businesses whose ads get spoofed could accuse them of being lazy hippies.

Meeting Magician
http://www.addictivemobile.com/blog/meeting-magician

Finally, something that offers no help for you at all. The free smart-phone app – there are iPhone, Android and Blackberry versions – passes time in dull meetings. 'Having spent 3 years at Mindshare/WPP either in meetings, on conference calls or on planes, I reckoned people needed some way to ease the pain of this way of life,' says the developer. It offers a word of the day to slip into conversation, lets you play buzzword bingo, work out how much the meeting is costing by calculating the time wasted from the salaries of the participants, and even lets you set up a fake emergency call to pull you out of the dullest meetings.